THE POET'S THIRD EYE

THE POET'S THIRD EYE

A Guide to the Symbolisms of Modern

Literature

by

Gordon E. Bigelow

Philosophical Library
New York

Copyright, 1976, by Philosophical Library, Inc.
15 East 40 Street, New York, N.Y. 10016
All rights reserved
Library of Congress Catalog Card No. 76-15706
SBN 8022-2188-2

Manufactured in the United States of America

This one is for the future:

Susan, Constance, Hal, Mark

CONTENTS

I conducted reconnaissance for what became chapter five of this book in two previously published essays: "The Problem of Symbolist Form in Melville's 'Bartleby the Scrivener,' " *Modern Language Quarterly*, 31 (Sept. 1970), 345-358; "Thoreau's Melting Sandbank: Birth of a Symbol," *International Journal of Symbology*, 2 (Nov. 1971), 7-13. I gratefully acknowledge generous assistance of several kinds from the Graduate School of the University of Florida, especially a research grant in the summer of 1970 which helped me to negotiate the formidable area of the theory of myth.

The unpayable debt, as always, is to my wife, Lydia, who in so many ways held the hand that held the pen.

G. E. B.

University of Florida, Gainesville
April 1976

INTRODUCTION

This is a kind of book which I wish someone else had written years ago so that I could have had it to use when I first began the serious study of literature. It is meant to be a kind of reader's friend and guide to the major phases of the symbolist tradition in modern literature. This tradition is so central to the literature of the last 100 years that it is something every student of modern culture should know about. And yet most discussions of symbolism are so narrowly specialized or are so scattered that a lucid account of the tradition as a whole is hard to come by. That is the kind of account I mean to provide here.

Our whole age appears to be haunted by the talismanic word "symbolism" in the same way that the eighteenth century was haunted by "reason" or the nineteenth by "science," and literary study in our time has been greatly enriched, and greatly confused, because it has imported widely varying meanings for this talismanic word from other fields such as philosophy, psychology, and anthropology. There are considerable differences in symbolism conceived of as a literary movement in late nineteenth century France and symbolism conceived of as theory of dream interpretation, or as a theory of knowledge, or as myth, or as a synonym for modernism. Yet in literary criticism the word has been asked to cover all these and more, to our general and very considerable confusion. In this book I have tried to discriminate between a number of these symbolisms as one stay against confusion.

One must somehow confront the problem of defining his key term. It will not do to say simply that the book as a whole is an extended essay in the definition of symbolism (though it is that), and so I have provided here in an appendix a generous gathering of definitions and observations on the nature of symbolism by thoughtful writers from several fields. These should prove enlightening in some ways and obfuscating in others, which is the way symbolism itself usually works upon the rational mind. In any case, they should serve to dramatize how complex and various an area of meanings symbolism really does cover in literary studies.

In keeping with my descriptive aim, I present relatively little new material here, but have tried to be content with faithful and objective exposition. There are two main exceptions. In Chapter V, "Myth as Literary Symbol," I distinguish "literary" from "functional" myth, and on the basis of this distinction argue several conclusions about the symbolic uses of myth. I have adopted also a somewhat broader meaning than usual for the term "symbolist." The word is commonly used in criticism to refer to the literary manner of a group of poets who are seen as forming an active second wave of the Romantic movement, beginning with the French symbolists of the 1880's and culminating in their immediate successors such as Eliot, Joyce, and Stevens. I find this conception too narrow because it excludes an important group of American symbolist poets of the last century who came before the French, and because I see no end so far to the symbolist manner in either poetry or prose. Consequently, I use the term "symbolist" to refer to any writing in any time or place which exhibits to a significant degree the principles of symbolist form described in Chapter V.

I have learned one thing for certain after a number of years hallooing through the great swamp after these various symbolisms, and that is that any inquiry into the nature of symbolism is an incursion into the irrational which means that there are going to be some portions of this material upon which no logical order can be imposed. I have also learned that though the chase can be full of excitement it is not without its dangers. The study of symbolism inevitably leads one into other dimensions of the irrational such as the grotesque, the absurd, the existential, the occult, and it therefore has a way of sending tremors of shock through one's most cherished assumptions about the nature of truth. Too much unwary exposure to the irrational of any sort can fry the brains, as Don Quixote learned from reading too many medieval romances. And I suspect that if anyone ever really caught up with symbolism he might find that he had caught a Lorelei whose embrace would seem like a *Liebestod* because it would mean abandoning so many of his favorite beliefs.

But on the other hand I am tempted to agree with Cassirer and Langer that the current obsession with symbolism may be the sign of a new stage of growth in human consciousness, and I feel that the rewards of a dalliance with symbolism are more than worth the risks, especially for the serious student of literature. Modern theories of symbolism have provided powerful means for restoring to literature a dignity and worth which it had seemed in danger of losing to empirical science. And the insights into poetic truth and the poetic process which the several symbolisms can provide seem to me as rich as those from any other source whatever.

CHAPTER ONE

From Allegory to Organism: A Map of the Terrain

I

Much of the present meaning for the word "symbolism" in literary studies was established nearly two centuries ago by the usage of Goethe, Coleridge, and certain other Romantic critics. The word as they used it meant *organic* symbolism of a particular kind which they defined from the very first in terms of contrast with allegory of a particular kind. Ever since that time, their definition of symbolism and their way of distinguishing it from allegory has carried the force of critical dogma, so that most discussions of symbolism in literature to this day are based upon a number of assumptions, usually unspoken and sometimes unrecognized, which include the following: (1) that allegory is a static or mechanic form and leads to poetry in an abstract mode and is therefore "bad"; (2) that symbolism is a living form and leads to poetry in an organic mode and is therefore "good"; (3) that allegory is a product of the fancy or some lower order of the imagination, while "symbolism" is a product of the highest order of the creative imagination; (4) that allegory is rational, ideological, or conceptual, and has definite paraphrasable meaning, while "symbolism" is mythic, dark, and mysterious with multiple suggestive, ambiguous, or paradoxical meanings. This critical dogma, in a word, while placing all faith and trust in a new organic symbolism, sees

1

allegory as *mere* allegory and by implication denies it status as a proper symbolism.

Now since most of the Western world's most illustrious literature was produced under the aegis of this older discredited mode of literary symbolism, it should be worthwhile to look into the reasons why it was suddenly dispossessed in favor of organic symbolism. Literature has always been symbolic in the general sense that it makes use of a symbolic medium of words and mediates in some fashion between the inner world of the human mind and whatever other world, physical or spiritual, lies outside the mind. But it is only in the early nineteenth century that symbolism becomes a major topic in literary criticism, and only in the later nineteenth and early twentieth centuries that it furnishes the basis for an important theory of knowledge, a new esthetic theory, and new dimensions to logic, anthropology, and psychology.

In the present essay I shall give a brief account of how this came about, emphasizing only main lines of development. My purpose will be to produce a kind of map of the difficult terrain of literary symbolism, and if the air seems thin for a time because of the high abstraction, we shall soon enough descend to the swamps and thickets of symbolism's lower landscape, where we shall be able to find our way with less stumbling because we shall carry in our minds a planform of the ground we must traverse. Cosmology can provide a convenient means of organizing a heterogeneous body of material, and for that we turn to a brilliant little book entitled *The Idea of Nature*,[1] in which R. G. Collingwood describes three world views which have served the Occident as controlling pictures of the world from early Greece to the present day. We shall follow Professor Collingwood in these three and then add a fourth from other sources. We should recognize at the outset the need for caution when viewing literature through the prism of cosmology, because world views are indistinct shapes at best and succeed one another only very gradually, even in times of swiftest change. Ideas or images which affect one man or one part of a society may have little effect on other men or other parts of that same society, and conflicting world views have a way of existing together in the same era and often in the same mind with mutual insouciance. Still, for our present purpose, cosmology can provide a useful way of describing the general tone and limits of the intellectual climate in different historical periods.

So we begin with the world of allegory, which is above all a world of stable *order*, and which for two milleniums was also an *organic* order, though its organicism was of a different kind from that of the modern world.

(1) *The Animate Universe*

The world view which prevailed from early Greek times through all of classical antiquity, the Middle Ages, and much of the Renaissance, says Collingwood, was based on an analogy to the human body. Men noted as they viewed their own bodies an organism made up of many individual parts moving in constant rhythmic fashion, delicately adjusted to one another so as to preserve the harmony and vitality of the whole. They were aware of a life-plan, a principle of growth or "soul," and they noted an intelligent mind which directed the body in its activities. This same pattern they then simply projected upon the universe, so that the entire universe was seen as animate, a macrocosm corresponding in specific detail to the microcosm of man, having a physical body, a soul or life-plan, and a rational intelligence governing the entire organism. All plants, animals, and objects in the natural world were thought to participate in the world-body—an idea not unfamiliar to the modern mind. But another assumption was also made—that all things participate in the world-soul and the world-mind, an idea of psychic correspondence quite alien to the modern mind. Often a third realm was interposed between man as microcosm and the universe as macrocosm, a middle realm which was sometimes seen as the entire terrestrial globe, the "geocosm," as it was happily named by Marjorie Nicolson;[2] or as the hieratic state, the entire body politic ruled by a divinely ordained king. Or sometimes the three worlds were described as earth, heaven, and the invisible world of spirit, with man understood to be the meeting place or mirror of all three. In all of these cases, man's relationship to the cosmos was assumed to be intimate, his every word or deed affecting the farthest reaches of heaven, and his own inner being open to interpretation by reading the stars or the configurations of earth.

A passage from Paracelsus, a sixteenth-century German-Swiss physician and alchemist, can illustrate the extraordinary lengths to which the idea of correspondence was sometimes carried: "Man is the lesser, and for his sake the Macrocosm, the greater world, was founded. . . .This therefore is the condition of the Microcosmus, or smaller world. It contains in its body all the minerals of the world. Consequently, the body acquires its own medicine from the world. There is a vast variety of things contained in the body of the Microcosm which elude the observation of the senses, though God, the Creator, has willed them to exist in that structure. There are, for example, more than a thousand species of trees, stones, minerals, and metals. . . ."[3] Paracelsus, like other physicians of his time, used such presumed correspondences between the human body and the world body as the basis for the healing arts.

Other cosmological images were also used to visualize the universe during these long centuries, such as the Great Chain of Being, according to which all creatures are ranged in a scale from highest angelic being to lowest worm, with man occupying a strategic level between earthly and heavenly creatures; the nine concentric crystalline spheres of Ptolemy; the image of the Cosmic Dance, in which the entire creation was pictured as moving in divinely ordained rhythmic patterns. But such images were usually harmonized, sometimes only with considerable ingenuity, with the fundamental concept of the universe as a living animal.

For the Middle Ages and the early Renaissance, we must add to this picture an overlay of the Hebrew idea of creation and several other specifically Christian doctrines. The Church did not question the assumption of an animate universe, but taught that this was the creation of God, who both indwelt His creation and held it in providential care, and also existed in some place outside and above it. Everything in the world, and most particularly man, for whom it had all been created, was thought to *belong* to God and to depend intimately upon Him for existence. The entire natural order was thought to speak, each part in its own way, of the glory of God, each part acting as a type of some divine attribute. Because of this participation in God's being and in the revelation of His truth, the entire world from pebble to star was conceived of sacramentally, as means to the salvation of men's souls. "The spirit was created for God's sake," wrote Hugo of St. Victor in the twelfth century, "the body for the spirit's sake, and the world for the body's sake, so that the spirit might be subject to God, the body to the spirit, and the world to the body"[4]. On all the altars of Christendom, God's concern for man and for the created universe was certified by His daily re-enactment of the Incarnation, in which the godhead became the humble and familiar substance of the bread and wine of the Eucharist.

If a modern man could enter the consciousness of a person living within this world view, he would be struck by the closeness of earth and heaven to his own being, by a poignant sense of personal involvement and belonging, by the concreteness and tangibility of his world, which would seem much more than usual within his own human scale and potential. Not that he would necessarily feel more comfortable or reassured, for if the heavens arched above his head in splendid shining spheres, hell just as surely flamed beneath his feet. Certain specifics of the elaborate correspondences between his own body and the world-body might strike a modern man as mere silliness or as fantastic nonsense, but these same correspondences would permit no idea of his own separateness and no idea that the material substance of earth or sky could be inert or dead or anything but *living* after the fashion of his own body. The whole world of spirit would have an extraordinary tangibility for these same reasons, and his own sense of involvement in the larger dimensions of psychic reality, angelic and demonic, would be continuous and vivid. He would find it quite reasonable to patronize astrology, or numerology, or other occult systems based upon the assumption of correspondences between his own person and the cosmos. Above all, he would be aware of living in an order which was remarkably stable, dependable, and unified.

The mode of literary symbolism which grew naturally out of this world view is *allegory*—a rich and many-faceted symbolism which, after a long period of neglect, has only recently begun to be rehabilitated.[5] Here, our purpose of sketching a grand design requires that we give only brief treatment to the theory of allegory and a description of several of its chief varieties.

Allegory flourishes on precisely those conditions just described—a stable order of existence made up of a hierarchy of levels or planes of differing quality or characteristic, but intimately related by the law of analogy as expressed in detailed systems of correspondence. All symbolism of whatever kind shares the principle of *mediacy*, and allegory in literature is an order of words mediating between two or more fixed categories of existence as a notation of some correspondence between them. Allegory lends itself easily to dualism and

5

perhaps for that reason, too, has been a familiar mode of thought and expression during much of the Christian tradition, which has felt strong attraction to such dualisms as the Platonic and the Manichaean.

Platonism, with its assumption of a transcendent realm of changeless Ideas and a changing physical realm which imperfectly reflects those ideal forms, has been especially strong in predisposing to allegorical expression in the arts. The following can illustrate the persistence even in the present century of the Christian *contemptus mundi* and the Platonic impulse toward allegory. It is a paraphrase of an introduction by Ralph Adams Cram, a well-known church architect, to a book entitled *Church Symbolism* (1938):

The absolute, the ultimate Truth which lies behind the show of things, can be apprehended or expressed only through the symbol. Man can touch or see only the outer fringes, the deceptive phenomena of reality. By his very nature, because of the limitations of his sensibilities, he is forever (within the limits of earthly life) debarred from direct contact with eternal Verity. The Absolute Truth is like a flame which would not vitalize but destroy. As in the classical myths, only the mirrored reflection is harmless. Whenever we try to express this Absolute, we can do so only by means of these similies familiar to us in life, the partial approximation, the creative and stimulating analogy, the Symbol. That is why we have art in all its varied forms, for in its highest aspect and function art is the symbolical expression of otherwise inexpressible ideas. Art is a manifestation of Beauty, which is neither personal nor variable. Neither personal taste nor changing fashion can make the parabolic curve of a Doric capital or a Gothic moulding other than beautiful, or a cubist sculpture or post-impressionist still-life or an art-nouveau apartment house other than ugly. In some mysterious way there is kinship or analogy between this visible beauty and the underlying truth of creation.[6]

Such confident and uncompromising assertions have about them the air of religious dogma, and, as it turns out, a strong reminiscence of medieval sacramentalism, for Mr. Cram goes on to urge the architect to design his church in such fashion that every part, from cruciform floor-plan to trifoliate window, can serve as the outward and visible sign of some inward and spiritual grace.

It was this same underlying sense of correspondence between the material and the immaterial worlds which informed the medieval theory of "types." In the context of Christian faith, where the whole

6

natural order was seen as participating in God's plan of creation and providence, everything pointed allegorically to God, and there were quite literally sermons in stones. The early Middle Ages, wrote Étienne Gilson, saw the whole earth as a kind of Bible, where things served as words. "Bestiaries, mirrors of the world, stained glass, cathedral porches, each in its own way expressed a symbolic universe in which things taken in their very essence are merely so many expressions of God."[7] Many remnants of this typology survive to the present day, such as the association of animals with traits of character, in a fashion reminiscent of the bestiaries—the fox with cunning, the lion with courage, the elephant with memory. There was a "language of flowers," as in Ophelia's distribution of flowers in Hamlet—rosemary for remembrance, pansies (pensées) for thoughts, fennel for flattery, columbine for ingratitutde, rue for sorrow, daisy for infidelity, violets for fidelity. And there was a similar symbolic "language" of trees, of herbs, and of precious stones.

In Biblical typology, the great structure of Christian doctrine and tradition served as a basic fixed category of an allegorical interpretation of Holy Scripture. Events and persons in the Old Testament, as construed by Christian doctrine, were read as types of something in the New Testament—Joshua or David were seen as types of Jesus' messianic leadership, Elijah's translation into heaven in a fiery chariot as a type of Jesus' Ascension. The problem of this kind of allegory was to discover the divine truth assumed to be present in words that also served the mundane purposes of history, law, or literature. The erotic love poetry of *Song of Solomon* and such ethical irregularities as Lot's behavior with his daughters, or David's legal murder of Uriah and the taking of his wife Bathsheba, offered serious but not insuperable challenges to ingenuity to be harmonized with Christian dogma by allegorical means. St. Augustine, for example, using an ingenious shuffling of etymologies and Biblical allusions, dealt with the David and Bathsheba story by equating Bathsheba with Holy Church, Uriah with Devil, and David with the Lion of Judah or God's Surrogate, and derived the following moral allegory: "Yet likewise He [God, in the form of David as the Lion of Judah], the desired of all nations, was enamoured of the Church bathing upon the roof, that is cleansing herself from the filth of the world, and in spiritual contemplation surmounting and trampling on her house of clay; and knowledge of her having been had at their first meeting, He afterwards killed the

7

devil [Uriah], apart from her, and joined her to himself in perpetual marriage."[8] Although the structure of Christian doctrine shifted somewhat with the Reformation, such allegorical habits of thought persisted, becoming more prevalent, if anything, in the Bible-based evangelical tradition, as witness Bunyan's *Pilgrim's Progress*, or the Bible sermons from present-day evangelical pulpits.

Classical rhetoric furnished the Middle Ages and the Renaissance with several other versions of a theory of allegory. The first of these described allegory simply as one of the tropes, along with irony, metonymy, synecdoche and metaphor. A trope (Gk., turning) is a rhetorical figure which says one thing while meaning another, and depending upon context and the poet's intention, can function either as central scheme of organization or as a rhetorical embellishment. From very ancient times this ongoing pattern of metaphor took the form of personification, as in Aristophanes' representations of the Good Logic and the Bad Logic in *The Clouds*, or Virgil's frequent depiction of such figures as Alecto the goddess of Discord. The same impulse is present without change in the late eighteenth century in such poems as William Collins' "Ode To Evening" where the evening is depicted as a nymph, a quiet maid with dewy fingers and dusky veil, with tresses bathed by spring showers, and a lap filled with autumn leaves.

C.S. Lewis in *The Allegory of Love* finds the *psychomachia* or *bellum intestinum* to be the classic subject-matter of allegory. He notes that the tendency to express what is immaterial in picturable terms seems to be a universal trait of the human mind, and notes also that there are two ways to use this correspondence between the two worlds. One can move from an immaterial but experienced fact such as the passions to concrete images of personification, as in the following: "If you are hesitating between an angry retort and a soft answer, you can express your state of mind by inventing a person called *Ira* with a torch and letting her contend with another person called *Patientia*."[9] Or one can move the other way, from sensible fact to an abstract or spiritual idea, for example, from the experience of a quiet evening to the idea of Peace and Tranquility. Professor Lewis would allow only movement in the first direction the name of allegory. Movement in the second direction he called "sacramentalism," or, confusingly, "symbolism," though he seems to be alone in enforcing such a distinction. We shall see that it may be the way in which the material and immaterial worlds themselves are conceived, and the nature of the correspondence assumed to exist between them, which determine whether or not allegory is present.

Most theories of allegory recognize a high degree of rational control or a high degree of abstraction in the concepts which are its usual subject-matter, as well as a high degree of artifice or stylization in the images with which it expresses these concepts. The notation of correspondence in allegory can be overt, as in Bunyan's didactic personifications Mr. Worldly-Wise-Man or Mr. Facing-Both-Ways; but it can also be covert, as in the use which Joyce made of the Odysseus myth in *Ulysses*. The double-speak of allegory gives it obvious usefulness to the satirist, the wit, or the ironist, as well as to the moralist.

A second mode of allegory deriving from classical rhetoric has been described in a distinguished recent book by Michael Murrin entitled *The Veil of Allegory*.[10] This is the allegory associated with the highest orders of poetry which was understood to be a version of the speech of the gods, that dark speech of oracles and prophets which contains divine truth in the form of riddle or enigma. In this kind of allegory, the poet is seen as a *vates*, a visionary prophetic figure who is seized in *furor poeticus* by the divine afflatus and speaks his vision of truth in deliberately veiled form. The veil of allegory, or the "dark conceit," as Spenser called it, is used with the double purpose of shielding divine truth from the profane multitude who are unable to grasp it, and at the same time making it available to an elite few who can penetrate to the true meaning beneath the veil. Dante's *Divine Comedy* and Spenser's *Faerie Queene* are only two among many major poems written in this mode. Allegory of this sort, because it intends to set forth ultimate truth which can never be perfectly understood by human reason, is presumed to be open-ended in meaning and demands interpretation at a number of levels. This is the kind of allegory which Dante in the letter to Can Grande called "polysemous," having the well-known four levels—the *literal*, setting forth the obvious meaning of the text; the *allegorical*, having to do with Christ's redemptive mission on earth; the *moral* or *tropological*, setting forth some moral doctrine having to do with man's inner life; and the *anagogical*, having to do with the four last things or God's eternal kingdom.

Helen Flanders Dunbar describes this "polysemous" kind of allegory as a highly sophisticated instrument of thought, leading to what she called "insight symbolism." "The question is never 'either-

9

or,' " she wrote, "but always of all meanings as true at once. The meaning on each higher level both includes and illuminates the lower, but never in any sense falsifies them. All meanings are necessary to an understanding of the fact in its universal implications."[11] Allegory of this kind is obviously at a far remove from the kind represented by a simple fable, and clearly it is far from the kind which Coleridge had in mind when he began his famous definition of organic symbolism by describing allegory as "a translation of abstract notions into picture language."

The allegory which made prophetic use of the dark conceit reached its apogee and its end in the English tradition, according to Murrin, in Spenser's *Faerie Queene*. Thereafter, such critics as Sidney and Ben Jonson, because they no longer took literally the poet's invocation of the divine muse, or saw his function to be the imparting of divine truth, understood the whole use of the veils of allegory to be superfluous, no more than an inflated form of ornate speech. The beginning of the age of reason and the urge to clarity and the plain style were at hand. And this brings us to a second world view.

(2) *The Mechanical Universe*

Beginning in the sixteenth and early seventeenth centuries, because of developments in scientific thought associated with such men as Copernicus, Galileo, and Newton, the picture of an animate universe seen as a macrocosm intimately corresponding to the microcosm of man began to give place to an entirely different world view, one which was based upon a wholly different analogy. This view denied the ancient assumption that the world is an intelligent organism with a soul and a body resembling those of man and claimed instead that the world is a vast machine, devoid of both life and intelligence, designed and set in motion by an intelligence outside itself. In the early seventeenth century the philosophy of Descartes formalized the idea of a separation between matter and spirit, between the subjective world of a man's mind and the objective world of nature. The inner realm of *res cogitans* was presumed to answer to the principle of the "clear and distinct ideas" of mathematical reason; and the outer world of *res extensa*, comprised now of cold and lifeless objects from which all animate or sacramental meanings had been stripped away, was pre-

10

sumed to answer with mechanical necessity and regularity to the entirely different principle of "nature's laws."

As might be imagined, this bifurcation of nature into two separate realms had dramatic, if not traumatic, impact on the Western consciousness. Not that everyone in Europe all at once dropped the notion of an animate universe for a mechanist one, but shock and wounds there truly were. Majorie Nicolson has shown how deeply John Donne and his contemporaries felt the shattering effect of this new world view which suddenly "put all in doubt"; how the circle, which had been pervasive in medieval and early renaissance literature as an image of unified perfection began to disappear from poetry as the ancient world view came under question; how the efforts of Donne to make the old correspondences work out made his imagery seem strained, ingenious, and "metaphysical" to an eighteenth-century critic like Samuel Johnson, who lived inside the new mechanical world view.[12] Two hundred years after the *Discourse on Method*, Hegel could still say with some heat that Decartes had "chopped the universe in two with a hatchet." And as we shall presently see, dismay at the separation between inner and outer worlds, and various efforts to heal this separation, were among the strongest motivations of the whole generation of Romantic poets and critics.

Floyd W. Matson has shown in a recent book that the Newtonian world view and the image of the machine, once promulgated, spread with extraordinary swiftness. In early Cartesian days an uneasy balance was maintained between the *res cogitans* and the *res extensa*, but this balance soon swung over toward matter and immediately gained such momentum that the old analogy between man and the universe was exactly reversed. "The human self," wrote Matson, "originally the source of explanation for the workings of inanimate nature, came in the end to be explained in the mechanical terms of natural causation. The subject was now regarded as an object; the human world was mechanomorphized."[13] The image of the machine which had originated in the physical sciences, soon invaded the biological and social sciences as well, achieving a dominance which it maintained until well into the present century, when developments in microphysics began to undermine the faith in mechanism.

If we ask now what mode of symbolism in literature accompanied the mechanist world view, we must respond—a little surprisingly, in

11

view of the radical nature of the change in cosmology—the various forms of allegory more than anything else. The main reason for this appears to be quite simply that though a few persons of the intellectual élite were committed to the radically new ideas of the Enlightenment, many persons, including most of the poets, were not, and the literature itself on the whole reflects more conservative and traditional views. For another thing, Roman rhetoric continued to serve until the end of the 18th century, as it had done for 1500 years, as the chief source of literary theory. And if we look to the new cosmology itself, we see that even though the idea of an animate universe and of elaborate correspondences between the microcosm of man and the macrocosm of the universe had broken down, many other features of the older world view persisted, notably the idea of a hierarchy and of a fixed order of existence. If the upper half of the Great Chain of Being containing the angelic orders was pretty much abandoned, the lower half, on which physical creatures were ranged, was kept pretty much intact, as Pope's *Essay on Man* bears witness. If the idea of a great unity in the created world had been shattered by the Cartesian dualism, the idea of a harmonious order of another sort had not. God was still understood to be the creator of the universe and His great world-machine was pictured as turning with marvelous, and now mathematically predictable, regularity in cosmic harmony. If miracles, angels, and demons were no longer "according to reason," there still remained a strong residue of Platonism and Christian idealism, a fondness for general ideas, for "uniformitarian thinking," as Professor Lovejoy has it, and therefore much use of "types," of personification, of allegorical forms in literature. If there was considerable talk of Reason, of rules, of art as mirror of nature, there was very little talk of any kind about symbolism, and this absence is worth mentioning because such talk became a prominent and distinguishing feature of literary criticism under the third world view, to which we now turn.

(3) *The Evolutionary Universe*

The third cosmology which we shall consider first appears around the turn of the nineteenth century about the same time as the beginning of the Romantic movement, and is often closely associated with that movement. This world view represents, in briefest terms, a return to organicism, but with the significant addition of the idea of progressive

12

change. The idea of evolutionary change in nature arises, according to Collingwood, from analogy with a radically new sense of history which emphasized "the facts" of particular times, places, and events, and thus stressed the idea of change and development in human affairs. "Modern cosmology," he wrote, "could only have arisen from a widespread familiarity with historical studies, and in particular with historical studies which placed the conception of process, change, development in the centre of their picture and recognized it as the fundamental category of historical thought."[14] This kind of history, which appeared for the first time about the middle of the eighteenth century in the French encyclopedists, soon found expression in the new science of biology, and eventually became famous as the idea of "evolution." Each of the earlier cosmologies had recognized that the world of nature is in constant change, but had commonly regarded such change as cyclical, like the changes of the seasons; or as belonging only to the surface of things; or, as in the Middle Ages, as belonging only to that part of the creation below the circle of the moon which was "fallen." Emphasis was placed, rather, upon the eternal constancy and changelessness of the cosmic order at large. However much change could be observed on the surface of things, it was assumed that underneath lay a supporting substrate which was eternally the same. In the new organicism, that very substrate itself was understood to move under one's feet, and the new organicism was to be distinguished by such key terms as "growth," "process," "development," and "evolution."

Some idea of the difference between the older outlook and the one produced by the new historical sense can be gathered by recalling the practice of medieval and renaissance painters of depicting Biblical scenes using settings and costumes contemporary to the painter. A modern viewer looks at such paintings with a twinge because his historical sense tells him that the snow-covered streets of a north European peasant village and sixteenth-century costumes are not in accord with "the facts" of life in Bible times. But to the painter himself, who looked upon his Biblical topic as part of the changeless moral order of the universe, such anachronisms were insignificant. To him the clothing and the streets of his own village were as suitable as "types" expressive of the living truth of his Biblical subject as anything in the Holy Land itself. Such an outlook, it is worth noting, has much in common with the primitive, or "mythic" outlook

13

described by Cassirer and others, which is characterized by a similar timelessness and obliviousness to everything but the qualitative aspects of an experience.[15] "It is the historical mind, rather than the scientific," writes Susanne Langer, " . . . that destroyed the mythical orientation of European culture; the historian, not the mathematician, introduced the 'higher criticism,' the standard of *actual fact*. It is he who is the real apostle of the realistic age."[16]

The new organicism, imbued with this sense of historical change, produced at once a whole panoply of new attitudes and ideas about literary symbolism, a tangled and colorful cluster which we can now start to unwind. To begin with, we can look more closely at the distinction between allegory and symbolism which seems to have been made first by Goethe.[17]

Allegory vs. Symbolism

Goethe's theory of symbolism sprang from his idea of nature, which was pantheist and anti-Newtonian, closely resembling the *naturphilosophie* of Friedrich Schelling, whom he knew. In this view, God, or the Great One, is equated with nature and can be known to the human mind only fleetingly as revealed in particular natural objects or events. There is in this view no transcendent realm of the ideal which lies somewhere beyond; nature itself is the *final* fact. "Let no man look for anything back of the phenomena," he wrote, "They are themselves the teaching."[18] This makes of every *thing* in nature, every object or event, a symbol which in some way can be expressive of the Great One. Goethe also believed, as did Schelling, that the art object, the poem, is no mere imitation or mirror reflection of nature, but is itself a living thing, containing the same symbolic power as natural objects of revealing the *Universal*, and now we can understand why he felt it necessary to distinguish symbolism of this kind from what he thought of as allegory. "It makes a great difference," he wrote, "whether the poet starts with a universal idea and then looks for suitable particulars or beholds the universal in the particular. The former method produces allegory, where the particular has status merely as an instance, an example [i.e., as a "type"] of the universal. The latter, by contrast, is what reveals poetry in its true nature: It speaks forth a particular without independently thinking of or referring to a universal, but in grasping the particular in its living character,

14

it implicitly apprehends the universal along with it.''[19] On a later occasion, Goethe described allegory as a dream or shadow, and contrasted it with true symbol in which the particular represents the universal as a living revelation.[20]

A key word in both passages is the word *living*. In the cosmologies of the past, which had presumed a fixed order in the universe, the symbol was understood to mediate the temporal world of change with some timeless and changeless order of being, but in the new organicism, the symbol is understood to be *part* of that which it reveals, to share the ongoing, processive characteristic of nature as a whole. Goethe is obviously thinking of allegory here in its least rather than in its greatest form—as a kind of *exemplum* of an abstract idea rather than as the dark, prophetic speech in the polysemous form of Dante's great poem; and it would appear to be the static quality of the form, as much as anything, which leads him to think of it as *mere* allegory. We should note further that he bases his judgment on criteria which are psychological, upon events taking place inside a poet's mind rather than upon *a priori* considerations of any kind, and this, too, represents a major shift in the way of conceiving the symbolism of poetry.

The organic concept of the symbol is known to the English-speaking world chiefly through Coleridge, who was influenced by both Goethe and Schelling. Coleridge's strong hostility to mechanism and his enthusiasm for organicism can be clearly seen in his familiar distinction between mechanic and organic literary form in the *Shakespearean Lectures* of 1818:

> The form is mechanic when on any given material we impress a predetermined form, not necessarily arising out of the properties of the material;—as when to a mass of wet clay we give whatever shape we wish it to retain when hardened. The organic form, on the other hand, is innate; it shapes, as it develops, itself from within, and the fullness of its development is one and the same with the perfection of its outward form. Such as the life is, such is the form.[21]

"Mechanic," we need hardly add, Coleridge associates with allegory, and with Fancy, which is the lowest of his orders of the imagination. "Organic" he associates with symbolism and with the Primary or Esemplastic, the highest of his orders of the imagination.

15

He expands Goethe's distinction between allegory and symbolism by itemizing the various gradations in which something particular expresses something more universal, and by introducing the expressive metaphor of translucence: "Now an allegory is but a translation of abstract notions into picture language, which is itself but an abstraction from objects of the senses. . . .On the other hand a symbol . . . is characterized by a translucence of the special in the individual, or the general in the special, or of the universal in the general; above all by the translucence of the eternal through and in the temporal." Coleridge also describes the functional principle of the new organic symbol as *synecdoche*: "It [the symbol] always partakes of the reality which it renders intelligible; and while it enunciates the whole, abides itself as a living part in that unity of which it is the representative."[22] Again that word *living*. We can see here the beginning of that prevalent dogma in modern criticism which not only separates allegory out as a different kind of thing from symbolism, but also places it at the bad end of a value spectrum whose good end is occupied by organic symbolism. From here on, allegory will in theory represent that kind of poetic statement for which there is some abstract or paraphrasable equivalent, and which is therefore thought to be inferior to "true" poetry which has a uniqueness and concrete particularity which are beyond paraphrase.

The Ambiguity and Many-Sided Meaning of Symbolism

From the very beginning the organic theorists asserted that whereas the meaning of allegory is limited and definite, the meaning of symbolism is unlimited and indefinite, containing always an important dimension of mystery and ambiguity. This is a factor which Carlyle emphasized in his discussion of symbolism in *Sartor Resartus*: "Silence is the element in which great things fashion themselves together. . . .Speech is of Time, Silence is of Eternity. . . .Of kin to the so incalculable influences of Concealment, and connected with still greater things is the wondrous agency of *Symbols*. In a Symbol there is concealment and yet revelation: here, therefore, by Silence and by Speech acting together, comes a double significance. . . .In the Symbol proper . . . there is ever . . . some embodiment and revelation of the Infinite; the Infinite is made to stand visible, and as it were, attainable there."

16

In his excellent book *The Poetry of Experience* (1957), Robert Langbaum expresses the assumption common to modern criticism that symbolism as compared to allegory has an "unlimited meaningfulness": "In the allegorical poetry of the Middle Ages and Renaissance," he writes, "the symbol stands in a one-to-one relation for an external idea or system of ideas. But the modern symbol exists as an object for imaginative penetration. Although any number of ideas may be applied to it as problematical interpretations, its ultimate meaning is itself, its own 'life,' which is to say the observer's life inside it." This is the party line of modern criticism as it comes straight from Goethe and Coleridge, and it emphasizes the importance of the inner experience of the poet as the chief criterion of value. This claims that the symbolism in modern poetry is problematic in meaning because there has been a shift in the stance of the poet toward the objective world. Professor Langbaum develops the important thesis that poetry since early romantic times is based upon a "doctrine of experience," according to which the poet says in effect: *My experience* of objects is *primary* and comes before any idea or analytic reflection which I may have about objects and before any logical or rational category which science may have assigned to them. Such a poet is interested in what Hopkins called the object's *inscape* or *thisness* rather than in its *whatness*; his aim is to perceive the object as much as possible from the inside, and he does this by rendering his own experience of it with utmost particularity.

It is this aim, Langbaum goes on to say, which makes the differences between a symbol used by Dante and the same symbol taken over by T.S. Eliot. The three beasts, the purgatorial mount, and Beatrice in Dante point (if obscurely) to definite ideas; the three leopards, the winding stair, and the Lady in Eliot have a much more ambiguous and indefinite reference. "Eliot's symbols invite penetration as Dante's do not," he continues, "because Eliot's symbols put forth an atmosphere of unlimited meaningfulness . . . the atmosphere of that mysterious ground from which the symbol emerges in the poet's self and with which it communicates in the reader's self." [pp. 65-66]

There is a certain condescension in the assumption that the ground from which the symbol emerges in Eliot is somehow more mysterious than the ground from which the symbol emerges in Dante. A simpler way to put this might be to say that the ground from which the symbol emerges in Dante is characterized by a metaphysical and religious certitude which is lacking in Eliot, and that the unlimited meaningfulness of Eliot's verse is a function of the modern metaphysical and religious uncertainty. But however it originates, such unlimited and ambiguous meaning is an identifying characteristic of modern symbolism. Edgar Allan Poe and the French Symbolist poets made ambiguity, tenuousness, and indefiniteness a major tenet in their esthetic creed, and all twentieth-century discussions of symbolism, in philosophy, psychology, and literary criticism alike, have assumed the problematic nature of symbolic meaning.

Symbolism Associated with Myth

In modern criticism one finds myth so closely associated with symbol that the two words tend to run trippingly off the tongue as one—"mythandsymbol." This close association of the two terms begins with the early German romantics, who saw the mysterious realm of myth as the fertile ground from which true poetry springs, the mother-substance of the poetic art. They deplored the general lack of a common mythic substructure in modern society and urged greater use of the older myths, particularly the Greek, as the ideal subject-matter for literature. Schelling made an especially close identification of myth with symbol. His concept of the symbol, like Goethe's, involved the idea that the particulars of nature all are capable of revealing something of the Great One, when momentarily the general and the particular coalesce. Like most other theorists of myth, he recognized that because myth is a collective, traditional phenomenon, it has large general significance, universal meanings which it expresses with the concreteness and particularity of poetry. And so he regarded the events and figures of mythology as satisfying unusually well that intersection of the universal with the particular which characterized his idea of the symbol. From this point of view, then, the Venus of the myths would not appear to be a mere sign or representative of beauty, she would *be* beauty itself, a concrete manifestation which gives beauty the only mode of existence it can have. A hundred years later Wallace Stevens was to express this same idea in the poem "Peter Quince at the Clavier," where, after invoking the old biblical story of Susannah and the Elders, he says with a kind of inverted Platonism: "Beauty is momentary in the mind—/ The fitful tracing of a portal;/

18

But in the flesh it is immortal./ The body dies; the body's beauty lives./ So evenings die, in their green going,/ A wave, interminably flowing."[23]

The Romantic fascination with Greek myth was part of a more general passion for all things Greek, but as is well known, myths of many other kinds also began to receive new attention and currency at this time. Wagner would soon make Germanic myth a major substance of his music-dramas, and later in the century, myth would become the subject of intense study in anthropology, sociology, and psychology, thence to make its way into the literary theory of the present century.

Meaning as Process: Perspectivism

M.H. Abrams in *The Mirror and the Lamp* (1953) has made familiar the idea that the images representing poetry in literature and criticism began to change in the early nineteenth century from images of the mirror to those of the lamp or radiant sun or gushing fountain, suggesting a shift from the conception of poetry as a reflector of a given fixed reality to the conception of poetry as a gushing center of meaning. In the medieval and mechanist world views, where everything was understood to have been formed by the hand of God and to be held in His providential care, a poet, his poem, and the objective world of nature were all looked upon as having similar status as created things. But in the new organicism we can note a radical shift away from the assumption that God is the source of all being and all truth, toward an assumption that the individual poet with his god-like imagination *creates* his own version of reality. This idea was actually the resultant of two converging lines of thought. The first came from Kant's famous *Critique of Pure Reason* (1781) with its thesis that the mind, far from being the passive receptor of experience which Locke had presumed, is an active agent and imposes its own conditions (time, space and the other "categories") upon what it knows, and thus in a true sense participates in the creation of its world. The second line of thought involved the prevalent notion of organic process, variously expressed in metaphors of the seed, the unfolding leaf, the growing plant. And so Coleridge's favorite image of the poet's mind was of a growing plant, a plant which *grows into* its own conceptions—and those conceptions, it turns out, were understood to be *symbols*. The

19

romantic poet erases the separation between his own subjectivity and the objective world by thinking himself into the objects of that world. By exercise of his imagination, he brings those objects into existence within his own mind, and thus in a sense becomes those objects. "There was a child went forth every day," wrote Whitman, "And the first object he look'd upon, that object he became,/ And that object became part of him for the day or a certain part of the day,/ Or for many years or stretching cycles of years."

Professor Collingwood notes that the new organicism eventually healed the Cartesian dualism by placing between the categories of mind and matter a third category, *life*, the idea of ongoing process which moves always in the direction of improved adaptation to an environment. This meant that the Cartesian categories of substance, the *res cogitans* and the *res extensa*, were converted into the idea of *function*; the *esse*, says Collingwood, became the *fieri*. The literary version of this phenomenon involved the symbol—the image or the poem (and eventually the whole medium of language)—which was located between the subjective and objective poles of reality, a *tertium quid* containing something of the poet and something of the natural world but fused by the imagination into a new thing. Emphasis was thus displaced from the fixed, all-seeing eye of God, or the "one clear, unchanging light" of Reason, to the moving eye of the poet. "I tramp a perpetual journey," chanted Whitman. "I am afoot with my vision . . . What I assume you shall assume." The single, all-embracing perspective of changeless omniscience or of changeless Ideas, becomes now the private, personal, limited perspective of the individual poetic consciousness, whose basic condition is continuous movement or process of change.

As the century wore on, writers showed increasing fascination with the various forms of literary perspective and controlled narration, which presented what was understood to be a *version* of the world. Gradually during these years the author disappears beneath the surface of his story or poem, while the linguistic medium, the words themselves, come to be regarded as having a magical and mysterious creative power of their own.

We have seen that Goethe and Schelling understood the poem as a whole to be a symbol, an object cognate to the objects in nature and alive with the same power of objectifying, that is, symbolizing, the Universal. A poem might contain a symbol, like the albatross in

Coleridge's *Ancient Mariner*, but a poem was also understood to be symbolic as a whole, a separate new entity made of words. From here it is not far to bestowing upon words themselves, upon the whole medium of language, the same symbolic status. Words and things, words and poems, words and symbols, words and the Word. They begin to run together and to achieve a kind of equivalence. In Emerson they do so explicitly: "Words and deeds are quite indifferent modes of the divine energy," he wrote. "Words are also actions, and actions are a kind of words."[24] Whitman was even more explicit: "Were you thinking that those were the words, those upright lines? those curves, angles, dots?/ No, those are not the words, the substantial words are in the ground and the sea,/ They are in the air, they are in you . . ./ Human bodies are words, myriads of words/ (In the best poems re-appears the body, man's or woman's, well-shaped, natural, gay. . . .)"[25] A little later, Mallarmé would insist to Dégas that "a poem is made not of ideas, but of words," and in the present century the poet's function would come to be generally understood as "an adventure in discovery among the meanings of words," and literary art an exploration of the symbolic medium of language.[26]

Symbolism as the "New Key" in Philosophy

With the Kantian idea of the "creative" mind, the idea of organic process, and the fascination with the symbolic medium of language, we have all the elements essential for the modern philosophy of symbolism, what Susanne Langer in a widely-known book has called the "new key" in philosophy. There is no need for us to attempt a repetition of her labors here, but in keeping with our scheme of noting the major facets of symbolism we should trace out the general shape of this important development. Ever since Descartes, Western philosophy has been haunted by questions about the human mind: *what* can we know: *how* do we know what we know? and above all, how can the mind have any true knowledge of the material universe, which is assumed to be outside and wholly different from the mind? Among other things, the philosophy of symbolism is a theory of knowledge and provides answers to such questions.

Drawing upon the ideas of Cassirer, Whitehead, and Wittgenstein, among others, Mrs. Langer describes the exhaustion of the generative idea of Descartes, that division of all reality into inner experience and

21

outer world which had permitted the dramatic achievements of modern science, and asserts that in the present century a new generative idea has been born, an idea which changes the very questions of philosophy and thus the picture of reality which philosophy presents. The new idea is the universal idea of symbolism, an assumption that the most essential and characteristic human trait is an innate tendency to make and to use symbols. The human mind is no longer seen as a collecting point or as a switchboard, but as a transformer, ceaselessly converting sensuous data into concepts. Cassirer argues that this trait sets man apart from all other creatures: "In the human world," he wrote, "we find a new characteristic which appears to be the distinctive mark of human life. The functional circle of man is not only quantitatively enlarged; it has also undergone a qualitative change. Man has, as it were, discovered a new method of adapting himself to his environment. Between the receptor system and the effector system, which are to be found in all animal species, we find in man a third link which we may describe as the *symbolic system*. This transforms the whole of human life. As compared with the other animals man lives not merely in a broader reality; he lives, so to speak, in a new *dimension* of reality." [*An Essay on Man*, p. 24]

Cassirer was an avowed disciple of Kant and extended the Kantian principle of the "categories" to include a number of *symbolic* categories, among which he named science, mathematics, religion, law, myth, the arts, and most important of all, language. Because of these categories man lives less and less in a physical and more and more in a symbolic universe. Cassirer described these categories as "spiritual forms," as "organs of reality," and thought of them as symbols in the large sense because as he wrote in *Language and Myth*, "it is solely by their agency that anything real becomes an object for intellectual apprehension, and as such is made visible to us. The question as to what reality is apart from these forms, and what are its independent attributes, becomes irrelevant here." [p. 8] These spiritual forms are not copies of something else or versions of some transcendent reality like the Platonic Ideas, but rather, each is "a spontaneous law of generation, an original way and tendency of expression," a force which produces and posits a world of its own. "Man lives with *objects*," he wrote, "only insofar as he lives with these *forms*; he reveals reality to himself, and himself to reality, in that he lets himself and the environment enter into this plastic

22

medium, in which the two do not merely make contact, but fuse with each other." [p. 10]

In this last statement we can see clearly several important features of the philosophy of symbolism: (1) the focus upon a symbolic medium or form, such as language, art, or mathematics; (2) which is conceived of as autonomous (that is, having power to produce its *own version* of the real world); (3) which is plastic (that is, involved in ongoing process); (4) and which has power to dissolve the Cartesian dualism by bringing together both subjective and objective poles of reality in a new fusion within the enveloping form of the symbolic medium.

Logical Positivism

Symbolism is a broad enough principle that it brings together strange companions under the same blanket. In addition to the important theory of knowledge described above, which stems from neo-Kantian idealism, we have also in the modern philosophy of symbolism strong representation of the scientific, empirical tradition in Wittgenstein and the logical positivists of the so-called "Vienna Circle," who come to symbolism through logic, mathematics, and a fascination with "meaning" or the semantic dimension of language. The logical positivists assume that all of philosophy amounts essentially to a critique of language. "The limits of my language," wrote Wittgenstein, "mean the limits of my world." He argued that our linguistic structures are models of reality and that through words, "we picture facts to ourselves." He conceived of language as a *logical* analogue to the facts of experience, and sought to isolate the pure shape of that analogy so as to form the principles of a language which would be valid for all the sciences. His test was rigorously empirical: he would accept as "meaningful" only those words or groups of words having an immediate one-to-one relationship to objects or events in the physical world—that is, only locutions having referents which were publicly verifiable by empirical means. Hence the label "positivist." He would include such forms as "The dog is barking," or "The boy hits the ball with the bat," but would exclude other verbal expressions such as "God is love," or "The truth shall make you free." Such locutions, because they have no tangible referents, are unverifiable, and are therefore irrelevant or nonsensical.

23

Rudolph Carnap, who expanded certain of Wittgenstein's ideas in a book called *The Logical Syntax of Language* (1934), allowed two kinds of meaning to language—the picturing of "facts" as described above, and the expression of emotion in a manner analogous to laughing, crying, or cursing. This means that to the logical positivists much of philosophy, particularly metaphysics, and the greater part of poetic expression, are either irrelevant, or senseless, or are like the grunts, moans, or shrieks of emotion. Behind this rigorous position was the laudable aim of achieving greater clarity in human thinking and a reduction of the smokescreen, hot air, and pettifogging which characterize much of human discourse, but the indifference or outright hostility to poetic, metaphysical, and religious considerations is apparent. Logical positivism comes into literary criticism as an important dimension of the New Criticism through the early writings of C.K. Ogden and I.A. Richards, among others.

(4) *The Hermetic World View*

Throughout our discussion we have been skirting a fourth cosmology which has special relevance to literary symbolism, and that is the occult or hermetic world view. The word "hermetic" comes from Hermes Trismegistos, the Thrice-great Hermes who is associated with the Egyptian god Thoth, the patron god of writing, magic, and astronomy. Hermes Trismegistos is supposed to have inscribed a legendary tablet of emerald with thirteen apothegms containing in epitome the ultimate in worldly wisdom, a summary of the hermetic philosophy. Versions of this philosophy exist from so many times and places, ancient and modern, oriental and occidental, that it is often called the *philosophia perennis* or "perennial philosophy." It was central to the religious systems of ancient Babylon and Egypt, to the Greek mystery cults, to Alexandrian neo-platonism, to Buddhism and the yogic systems of India, to medieval alchemy, astrology and numerology, to Illuminism and the Masonic rituals, to Rosicrucianism, Swedenborgianism, and the various forms of mind-science and theosophy in the twentieth century. The following brief digest of the main cosmological features of the perennial philosophy has been paraphrased from chapter five of John Senior's excellent book, *The Way Down and Out: The Occult in Symbolist Literature* (1959):

The universe is One, comprised of a single, eternal, and ineffable substance, which manifests itself as spirit, fire, or light; or, working through the creative Demiurge or Logos, as the visible world. The created universe is composed of paired opposites—male-female; light-dark—which generate through dialectic process their own equilibrium or harmony. Things above (spirit) are the same as things below (matter), and knowledge of the one can be obtained from the other through the law of universal analogy. The image of the created world is the human body, and the universe itself is, in fact, a living man. Man is capable of becoming God, because in his true Self he is God, though he often does not realize it. The way of realizing his god-like nature is through self-knowledge, a penetration into the dark and unknown layers of the psyche, which is often symbolized as a descent into hell. All things live in cycles of birth, growth, and decay—the world in the thousand-year cycle of the Magnus Annus; man in the cycle of birth, death, and resurrection.

It can be seen at once that not only the pantheism of Goethe and Schelling but also many aspects of the medieval cosmology, including its idea of an anthropomorphic, animate universe, and its elaborate systems of correspondence, are essentially occult. But the received cosmology of Christendom, while basically occult until the seventeenth century, was not strictly so because of the overlay of Christian doctrine, which taught for instance that God is one, but did not permit the pantheism which was a natural extension of such a doctrine. Nevertheless the perennial philosophy in purer form maintained a continuous existence through the whole course of Western history, running either underground or parallel to the received forms of orthodoxy. During most of that time it was embodied in those familiar and slightly sinister figures of the sorcerer, the astrologer, and the alchemist, and since early Romantic times, in the poets. Hermetic ideas have been transmitted in the writings of the neoplatonists, especially Plotinus, in the Hebrew Kabbala, in the numerous alchemical writings, and in the writings of such persons as Jakob Boehme, Nicholas of Cusa, Meister Eckhardt, and the Cambridge platonists, and whenever such names are mentioned as part of an author's reading, one can be fairly certain that he has been exposed to occult ideas and attitudes. In the very midst of the Enlightenment, Emmanuel Swedenborg produced a version of the occult philosophy which had great influence on many of the most important writers of the nineteenth century, both in Europe and America. The Enlightenment itself, with its mechanist world-view and its scientific rationalism and empiricism, must be seen as a major break in the surface continuity of occultism in Western culture; and the Romantic movement must be seen among other things as a major effort to re-establish that continuity.

The strong attachment of Blake and Yeats to the occult is well known, but less well known is the fact that many other poets since the beginning of the Romantic movement are also occultists to an important degree. "The world view of the romantic movement," writes John Senior, "is occultism. At least insofar as romantic poets expressed philosophical and cosmological ideas, those ideas were occult. Consider just the greatest names out of thousands—Shelley, Blake, Hugo, Nerval, Gautier, Goethe, Novalis. . . .Occult ideas are involved with their greatest work."[27] A similar list of nineteenth-century American writers involved with hermeticism would include Poe, Emerson, Thoreau, Hawthorne, Melville, Whitman, Henry James, and possibly Emily Dickinson.

In the literature of the present century, hermetic ideas are to be found nearly everywhere—from W.B. Yeats and Wallace Stevens to T.S. Eliot and W.C. Williams, from Joyce and Conrad to Faulkner and Steinbeck. They are fed into our literature and criticism from many of the same sources as symbolism itself, in one line from Goethe and Coleridge, in another from Poe and the French Symbolists, in another from the American transcendentalists and Whitman, and more recently from the writings of C.G. Jung and a whole wave of "oriental" influences ranging from Zen Buddhism to acupuncture. There is good reason to agree with Professor Bertocci's remark that "the ancient occultist world view seems to crop up wherever there is symbolism, be it in Goethe, Baudelaire, Mallarmé, or Yeats."[28] And small wonder, for the occult pattern accommodates itself to the entire range of principles expressed in the other cosmological systems we have described. It allows for monism and for changelessness in the doctrine of the Great One; for evolutionary change in the doctrine of the Many and of the cycles; for hierarchy and dualism in the correspondences of "as above, so below"; for paradox and ambiguity in the principle of paired opposites.

Whatever other cosmological ideas may have been current, the continuous presence of these occult doctrines, underground or above ground, has furnished a potential theoretical basis for symbolism throughout the entire course of Western literary history. This is especially true of the doctrine of ''as above, so below,'' which permitted systems of correspondence between the spiritual and the physical worlds, and the doctrine of the Great One which led to versions of the universal analogy, whereby any single aspect of the universe can be related to any other. It is because of a common participation in such doctrines that the older polysemous allegory of the dark conceit and the newer organic symbolism both tend to converge toward a single symbolic principle. And it is for this reason that symbolism in literature, from a cosmological perspective, appears to be not many but one, a coat of many colors, perhaps, but ultimately one. To pull on any single thread of this garment means before long to unravel the whole garment. Goethe and Coleridge pulled on the thread called ''symbolism'' and made allegory virtually disappear; and in more recent years, Edwin Honig and Angus Fletcher have pulled on the thread called ''allegory'' and have made ''symbolism'' virtually disappear.

But it is reasonable to ask, are there no differences, then, between allegory and ''symbolism?''—Or do they simply merge far away in Baudelaire's ''shadowy and profound unity?'' The answer must be a discomfiting paradox: yes, they do merge in a single principle, and yes, there are substantive differences between them. Modern symbolism has two wholly novel characteristics which, when emphasized, distinguish it from older symbolisms of the allegorical kind: (1) it is for the first time symbolism which has become self-conscious, and (2) it is symbolism imbued with the modern time sense.

In the cosmologies before the romantic era, symbolism seems to have been taken more or less for granted as a given part of a given world order, a function of relatively stable systems of correspondence which articulated all parts of that order. After the romantic era, the conscious fascination with the symbolic process became an obsessive part of the mind's attempt to know the secrets of its own functioning, and there was an explosive proliferation of symbolism in many areas: a major symbolist movement in American literature at mid-century; another much-more-publicized symbolist movement a little later in French literature; the mythic music-dramas of Wagner; the intensive study of myth by philologists, folklorists, and social scientists of several sorts; the systematic, empirical study of dream symbolism by Freud and his followers; the recognition of symbolism as a new

27

"generative idea in philosophy." Conscious symbolism became, in a word, a hallmark of the modern sensibility, and has often been used as a kind of code word for the whole modernist manner in literature and the arts, just as "allegory," after Goethe and Coleridge, has been a code word for an older sensibility and literary manner.

The second wholly new trait of modern organic symbolism is its time sense, and this involves another paradox. We have noted that organic symbolism represents an awakening from what Blake called "Newton's sleep," a recovery of certain ancient mythic attitudes which had been eclipsed for a time by the dazzling successes of the Enlightenment. And this means that modern symbolism is very old because it embodies such occult or mythic concepts as animism, pantheism, word-magic, and the universal analogy. Its time sense is, on the one hand, the ancient mythic timelessness, the cyclic recurrence of the Eternal Now of the Great One. "God culminates in the present moment," wrote Thoreau, "and will never be more divine in all the lapse of the ages." "There was never any more inception than there is now," wrote Whitman. "Nor any more youth or age than there is now./ And will never be any more perfection than there is now./ Nor any more heaven or hell than there is now." But on the other hand, the time sense of organic symbolism is very new because it acquired a new component from the empiricism of the Enlightenment. To use A.O. Lovejoy's word, it was "temporalized." And this means that at the same time that it expressed the ancient mythic timelessness, it also embodied the modern time sense which includes the linear idea of history, the idea of continous evolutionary progress, and the idea of relative or perspectival reality. The closed circle which symbolized unified perfection to the medieval world became the vortex, or the helix, the continually ascending spiral of modern evolutionary thought. "Some say existence," wrote Robert Frost, "like a Pirouot/ and Pirouette, forever in one place/ Stands still and dances, but it runs away,/ It seriously, sadly runs away/." William Carlos Williams caught the paradox of time as a stasis of the Eternal Now and time as endless flow in the image of the falls of the Passaic River at Paterson, where the rushing torrent of the river is momentarily combed into smoothness at the edge of the falls before it crashes onto the rocks below and flows off to the sea.

We should take note, finally, of the obvious fact that the great burgeoning of symbolism after the romantic breakthrough took place alongside an aggressive growth of positivistic science and an equally aggressive growth of literary realism and naturalism. And we should also take note of the fact that allegory continued a healthy existence quite as if it had never been separated out from "symbolism" and cast into opprobrium by the romantic critics. Allegory may be most at home in a world of fixed categories and stable systems of correspondence, but since the law of analogy operates quite as well in the new temporalized world order as in the old, allegory continues to enjoy an undiminished prosperity, as the writings of Joyce, Kafka, Orwell, Golding, and Barth are sufficient witness. In recent years allegory has less traffic with a priori or transcendental categories than in the past, and its main difficulty in a fragmented world would seem to be to find an audience, to locate categories large enough to encircle general rather than specific human experience. These seem to be mainly secular categories with a political or social cast, such as Orwell's exploration of the totalitarian state in terms of the behavior of barnyard animals, or Kafka's depiction of the nightmarish guilt and estrangement produced by modern bureaucratic society; though Golding, in *Lord of the Flies*, examines the old metaphysical problem of human depravity. One of the attractions of traditional myth to modern writers seems to be that it provides categories large enough and stable enough to be used as one end of an allegory, the most notable case being Joyce's use of the *Odyssey*.

One thing we see at the end of our cosmological vista is that allegory needs to be allowed back in the house as a legitimate symbolism, and that the long-standing binary formula of the romantic critics which sets allegory over and against "symbolism" might profitably be set aside. For we can now see quite plainly that both allegory and "symbolism" in their separate ways serve the essential function of the symbol. Both serve as the meeting place of opposing tendencies and principles where the timeless becomes temporal and the ineffable becomes knowable to the conscious mind; both serve to reveal something of those harmonious and conflicting truths of what Wallace Stevens called the "ever-never-changing same."

29

[1] *The Idea of Nature* (New York, 1960).

[2] *The Breaking of the Circle; Studies in the Effect of the "New Science" Upon Seventeenth Century Poetry*. Rev. ed. (New York, 1960). See also two other classic works which relate cosmology to literature: A.O. Lovejoy, *The Great Chain of Being* (Cambridge, Mass., 1936); and E.M.W. Tillyard, *The Elizabethan World Picture* (New York, 1944).

[3] *The Hermetic and Alchemical Writings of Paracelsus*, transl. by Arthur E. Waite (London, 1894)I, 161.

[4] Quoted in Henry Osborn Taylor, *The Medieval Mind* (London, 1938) 2 vols., II, 91-92. The entire Book V of vol. II of this work, entitled "Symbolism," is useful for its account of medieval allegory.

[5] Three important books on the theory of allegory appeared in the decade 1959-1969: Edwin Honig, *Dark Conceit: The Making of Allegory* (Evanston, Ill., 1959), six essays on a variety of topics in the history and theory of allegory; Angus Fletcher, *Allegory: The Theory of a Symbolic Mode* (Ithaca, N.Y., 1964), a rich *pot pourri* of a book, a heterogeneous study of allegorical theory and techniques including essays on character, style, themes, the relationship of allegory to ritual, psychoanalysis, the sublime and picturesque; Michael Murrin, *The Veil of Allegory: Some Notes Toward a Theory of Allegorical Rhetoric in the English Renaissance* (Chicago and London, 1969); in spite of the modesty of the sub-title, a brilliant study of allegory as the veil covering the divinely inspired truth which was the subject of the greatest poems of the Middle Ages and early Renaissance.

[6] F.R. Webber, *Church Symbolism*, rev. ed. (Cleveland, 1938).

[7] *The Spirit of Medieval Philosophy* (New York, 1936), p. 100.

[8] Taylor, II, 71.

[9] *The Allegory of Love* (London, 1936), p. 45.

[10] *The Veil of Allegory* . . . (Chicago and London, 1969).

[11] *Symbolism in Medieval Thought with Special Emphasis on Dante's 'Divine Comedy'* (New Haven, 1929), p. 21.

[12] *The Breaking of the Circle*, Chapter 1.

[13] *The Broken Image* (New York, 1966), p. 231.

[14] *The Idea of Nature*, p. 10. See also R.G. Collingwood, *The Idea of History* (London, 1946), p. 232, 321; and J.B. Bury, *The Idea of Progress* (New York, 1932), esp. ch. 7.

[15] For a more detailed discussion of this idea, see ch. 4 of the present study.

[16] *Philosophy in a New Key* (New York, 1951), p. 232.

[17] René Wellek, *A History of Modern Criticism 1750-1950* (New Haven, 1955), 4 vols., II, p. 17.

[18] Quoted in Karl Viëtor, *Goethe the Thinker*, Trans. by Baynard Q. Morgan, (Cambridge, Mass., 1950) p. 14.

[19]Quoted in Philip Wheelwright, *The Burning Fountain*, Rev. ed. (Bloomington, Ind., 1968), p. 54.

[20]Quoted in Erich Heller, *The Disinherited Mind* (New York, 1959), p. 161.

[21]"Shakespeare, A Poet Generally," *Complete Works*, ed. W.G.T. Shedd (New York, 1961), IV, 55.

[22]"The Statesman's Manual," *Complete Works,* ed. W.G.T. Shedd (New York, 1961), I, 437-8.

[23]*Collected Poems* (New York, 1964), p. 92.

[24]"The Poet," *The Works of Ralph Waldo Emerson*, ed. James E. Cabot (Boston and N.Y., 1883), III, 14.

[25]"A Song of the Rolling Earth."

[26]See Charles Feidelson Jr., *Symbolism and American Literature* (Chicago, 1953), ch. 2.

[27]*The Way Down and Out: The Occult in Symbolist Literature* (Ithaca, 1959), p. 50.

[28]Angelo P. Bertocci, *From Symbolism to Baudelaire* (Carbondale, Ill., 1964), p. 18.

CHAPTER TWO

The French Symbolist Movement

Spelled with a final -e, *symbolisme* refers to an important historical movement in French literature of the nineteenth century; the persons participating in the movement are commonly called the *symbolistes*.[1] So pervasive has been the influence of this group of poets on twentieth-century poetry and criticism that in some quarters "symbolism" and "symbolist" are assumed to have automatic reference to them. But it will help to avoid one level of confusion if we use the French terms consistently when referring to this movement and to these poets and save the English forms for broader and more inclusive usages. Like most such movements, this one is difficult to describe or to date with precision, but the following persons are usually regarded as belonging in some way to the group: Gérard de Nerval (1808-1855), poet, mystic, a precursor; Charles Baudelaire (1821-1867), often thought of as the "father" of the movement because of the great influence of both his poems and his critical writings: Villiers de L'Isle-Adam (1838-1889), novelist and playwright; Paul Verlaine (1844-1896), one of the important poets; Joris-Karl Huysmans (1848-1907), novelist and critic; Stéphane Mallarmé (1842-1898), the chief theorist and one of the important poets; Arthur Rimbaud (1854-1891), precocious poet and adventurer; Jules Laforgue (1860-1887), poet; Paul Valéry (1871-1945), disciple of Mallarmé, important poet and critic, and often considered the last of the direct line.

32

A glance at the dates of these men will show that in terms of the lives of the participants the movement ran for nearly a century, and it might be argued that in a general sense it is running still in the writings of this century. The list above is sparse and might include many more names such as those of Apollinaire, Corbière, Maeterlinck, Verhaeren, and of course Edgar Allan Poe, who, though not French, is universally honored by the French and by most literary historians as the "godfather" of the movement. *Symbolisme* was originally a distinctly Parisian movement, flourishing in the 1880's, but by the 1890's it had become an international literary phenomenon and eventually had important representatives in most literatures of the Western world. To list the twentieth-century poets descended from this group is to name the major poets of the century. Waves of influence from the *symbolistes* moved out to encircle not only poetry but drama and fiction as well, so that it is not an exaggeration to see in this movement one of the major sources of modern literary sensibility.

The chief purpose here is to describe the mode of symbolism espoused by these poets—not an easy thing to do, since they differed considerably from one another in both theory and practice. They did have, nevertheless, a number of attitudes and assumptions in common, and these gave their verse at least generic similarity, and set it apart from other poetry before them and around them. This makes it possible to formulate a set of representative doctrines and to draw the general shape of their kind of symbolism, so long as we understand that individual poets might depart significantly in particulars from the central design. The important theorists of the *symboliste* movement were Baudelaire, Mallarmé, and Valéry, all of whom openly acknowledged Poe as a primary source of their esthetic ideas. Baudelaire's translations and commentaries on Poe, made in the 1850's, were known to the two younger poets, but they also made independent study of Poe, and anyone familiar with the writings of the American poet will recognize the pervasive influence of his ideas in what follows.[2]

A number of scholars, including René Wellek and Edmund Wilson, believe that *symbolisme* is a resurgent second phase of the romantic movement. They claim that romanticism only went underground when realism and naturalism grew strong during mid-nineteenth century, then staged a powerful counter-revolution with the *symbolistes* in the 1870's and 80's. However that may be, there is no question that the *symbolistes* consciously set themselves against the prevailing scientism and materialism of their day, and against the realist techniques of the Parnassian poets such as Leconte de Lisle and Heredia and such novelists as Balzac and Zola. All of the *symbolistes* were Platonists or Neoplatonists and they assumed as the central doctrine of their esthetic creed the existence of an ideal beauty which lay behind the world of appearances. One function of poetry was to set forth or give access to this beauty in the sensible world. They are properly called *symbolistes* because they thought of their poems, in whole or in part, as symbolic of this supernal Beauty. Their own experience of beauty was sometimes ecstatic and visionary in the same sense that a religious person might have a mystic experience, and reference to the dream state is pervasive both in their poems and their critical writings.

Like other idealists, they believed that the transcendent perfection of the ideal could never be more than imperfectly realized on earth, and that it could best be invoked by indirect and suggestive means. "I think that things should be presented allusively," wrote Mallarmé. "Poetry lies in the contemplation of things, in the image emanating from the reveries which things arouse in us. The Parnassians take something in its entirety and simply exhibit it; in so doing, they fall short of mystery; they fail to give our minds that exquisite joy which consists of believing that we are creating something. To *name* an object is largely to destroy poetic enjoyment, which comes from gradual divination. The ideal is to *suggest* the object. It is the perfect use of this mystery which constitutes symbol."[3] The key terms here are *allusively, contemplation, mystery, divination*, and *suggest*. They contain a number of the important *symboliste* doctrines such as the opposition to Parnassian realism, and the assumption that poetry involves a *process*, an ongoing, contemplative experience, which makes great demands upon the reader, who must for himself, through the agency of the poem, enter a mysterious state of reverie or dream. In this visionary state, images arise which by analogy provide glimpses of the supernal beauty. The poet has entered this ecstatic state, the reader must also enter it to achieve the vision for himself. A true poem does not tell the reader about things, does not tell a story, does not talk about moral truth; it is instrumental; it gives him an experience. It provides a window through which he can glimpse the eternal; or it is a charm which has ensnared some part of the heavenly radiance and presents it living on the page.

34

Many of the *symboliste* conventions can be seen in the following poem by Verlaine:

Clair de Lune

Votre âme est un paysage choisi
Que vont charmants masques et bcrgamasques,
Jouant du luth et dansant et quasi
Tristes sous leurs déguisements fantasques.

Tout en chantant sur le mode mineur
L'amour vainqueur et la vie opportune,
Ils n'ont pas l'air de croire à leur bonheur
Et leur chanson se mêle au clair de lune,

Au calme clair de lune triste et beau,
Qui fait rêver les oiseaux dans les arbres
Et sangloter d'extase les jets d'eau,
Les grands jets d'eau sveltes parmi les marbres.

[Moonlight]

[Your soul is a rare landscape
Where charming masquers and shepherd mummers pass
Playing the lute and dancing, almost
Sad beneath their fantastic dress.

Even while they sing in minor key
Of love triumphant and of happy life
They seem not to believe their happiness
And their song melts into the light of the moon,

Into the calm light of the moon, sad and lovely,
Which sets the birds to dreaming in the trees
And makes the fountains sob in ecstasy,
The great fountains gushing slender streams amid
    the statues.][4]

A pleasant little poem, but how, exactly, is it *symboliste*? We can begin an answer by showing how it is *symbolic*, for only a relatively few of the *symboliste* conventions have to do specifically with symbol itself. We note first that although the poem is entitled "Moonlight" it is devoted mainly to describing an imaginary landscape, a kind of formal garden containing marble statuary and fountains which gush slender streams into the air. In this garden, pastoral masquers, fantastically costumed, dance and strum lutes and sing sadly of happy love. Everything is bathed in moonlight, which causes the birds in the trees to dream and the fountains to sob in ecstasy—altogether a landscape strongly reminiscent of the artifice of a Watteau painting and the gardens of Versailles. None of these particulars is a symbol in itself, but all taken together are symbolic of the soul of an unnamed woman. The whole poem is a kind of trope which, *by indirection*, describes this soul. But the poem's symbolic translucence does not stop here, for in and through this tenuous soul we also discern Beauty, as shimmering and tenebrous as the moonlight itself, and we sense the poet's own mood of bittersweet melancholy entangled in the elements of his visionary landscape. The ecstatic sobs of the fountains are his own, and the moonlit dreams of the birds, and the sad-happy songs of the mummers. This evanescent Beauty and the poet's mood are quite as much the "subject" of the poem as the soul of the woman is.

The importance of indirection to the *symboliste* method is particularly plain; we go from moonlight in the title to a visionary garden to a woman's soul to Beauty to the poet's own subjective emotion; and somewhere in this magic circle the Cartesian boundaries between subject and object have been dissolved. The poet's inner feeling and the external reality he depicts are completely intermingled. The poem's suggestiveness, its stress on ambiguous nuance of mood, its air of mystery, its musicality in the French original, its quiet intimate tone, its shunning of narrative, are all aspects of the poem which are conventions of *symbolisme*, though we should stress again that they are not in themselves symbols. It should be added that in this poem Verlaine is not following the advice he was later to give in his "Art Póetique," that the poet should keep his rime in check and let his lines run free. His rimes here are strong and his verses and stanza forms regular.

Behind the *symboliste* theory of poetry lay several hermetic or occult assumptions, the first of which can be expressed by the inscription on the legendary smaragdine tablet of Hermes Trismegistos: "Things below are as things above"; that is, there is a radical

36

correspondence between the physical and spiritual realms. Objects in the physical world have not only a phenomenal existence, but also, by analogy, give suggestive hints of the heavenly realm, as Verlaine's garden images are intended to arouse intimations of a heavenly Beauty. The arts are the aspect of human life most imbued with the mysterious power of analogy, and of the arts poetry, with its magic of metaphor, peers most deeply into the ineffable. The objection to naming things directly in poetry is that this overemphasizes the physical and appeals too much to the conscious reason. The spiritual can be perceived only by the "soul" and the soul can be appealed to best by various indirect means.

Of the means available to the poet to suggest rather than to name, to create the atmosphere, or to evoke the presence of some aspect of the physical world rather than delineate its physical outlines, music was of highest importance. "You must have music first of all," said Verlaine in his "Art Poétique," "And for that a rhythm uneven is best,/Vague in the air and soluble,/With nothing heavy and nothing at rest./" The *symbolistes* thought of music as "pure" art, the kind of art which is uncontaminated by reference to the world of phenomena. They observed that music can produce its most poignant effects without evoking any awareness of a tangible physical reality outside itself, or of a thematic or topical idea. They deliberately abandoned the centuries-old analogy between poetry and painting, the *Ut pictura poesis* of Horace, and sought to achieve a "pure" poetry in which words and poetic images would produce psychological or emotional effects similar to those of music. Toward the traditional rhetorical means of literary art, the prescriptions of grammar, syntax, style and the genres, they were quizzical or contemptuous. "Take eloquence," said Verlaine, "and wring its neck." They experimented with novel rime, meter, and stanzaic forms, and Mallarmé, at least, in a poem entitled "Un Coup de Dés" ["A Throw of the Dice"] tried radically novel typographical effects of the sort used later by such poets as Cummings and William Carlos Williams. Laforgue, who translated Whitman into French, is usually credited with introducing free verse into French poetry of this period.

The quasi-religious commitment to art of several of these poets, notably Baudelaire and Mallarmé, extended to a perfectionism in their craft resembling that of Flaubert. And this sometimes resulted in the paradox of a poetry which was committed to dream and evanescence yet which was produced by intellection, by the most meticulous and self-conscious devotion to technique. Mallarmé's urge to polish his poems was so compulsive that he often kept a poem at hand for years, seeking perfection of nuance. The small number of his·published poems is directly related to this obsession for perfection of surface.

A second occult assumption which underlay *symboliste* theory and practice was the idea that all things are One; particular things exist, but only as they participate in this great Unity. "*Tout vit,*" wrote Nerval, "*tout agit, tout se corréspond.*" "Everything lives, everything moves, everything corresponds."][5] Baudelaire wrote on a number of occasions of "the universal analogy," from whose inexhaustible depth the poet draws all his metaphors, similes and epithets. He believed that because all things are part of the great One, all things in some sense correspond, not only in the vertical sense, between matter and spirit, but also in the horizontal sense, between objects or aspects of the physical world. The frequent use of synesthesia in the imagery of the *symboliste* poets is one reflection of this idea. Baudelaire's famous sonnet "*Correspondances*" can provide an ideal illustration since it gives both theory and example. As we read the poem we need to remember the tactical assumption of the *symbolistes* that reason must be lulled or baffled so that reverie can be induced and "feelings" rather than thoughts aroused. The first quatrain of this sonnet has that unhinging effect by establishing an atmosphere which is at the same time sacral and eerie, in which the roles of subject and object have become strangely reversed. Instead of the pattern familiar to romantic tradition of the lordly ego contemplating or moving with masterful dominance through a beautiful but passive nature, we have here a nature which is conceived as the active, living agent, a temple of living trees, a forest of symbols, peering with an air of knowing sufferance at the strangely passive man. The confusion of images and of viewpoint is a counterpart of the confusion of words which seem to issue from the forest rather than from the man:

Correspondances

La Nature est un temple où de vivants piliers
Laissent parfois sortir de confuses paroles;
L'homme y passe à travers des forêts de symboles
Qui l'observent avec des regards familiers.

38

Comme de longs échos qui de loin se confondent
Dans une ténébreuse et profonde unité,
Vaste comme la nuit et comme la clarté,
Les parfums, les couleurs et les sons se répondent.

Il est de parfums frais comme des chairs d'enfants,
Doux comme les hautbois, verts comme les prairies,
—Et d'autres, corrompus, riches et triomphants,

Ayant l'expansion des choses infinies,
Comme l'ambre, le musc, le benjoin et l'encens,
Qui chantent les transports de l'esprit et des sens.

[Correspondences]

[Nature is a temple from whose living pillars
Confused words at times emerge;
Man passes through this forest of symbols
Which observe him with familiar glances.

Like prolonged echoes which merge far away
In a shadowy and profound unity,
Vast as the night and as the light,
Perfumes, colors, and sounds answer one another.

There are perfumes fresh as the flesh of children,
Sweet as oboes, green as the prairie,
—And others, corrupt, rich and overpowering,

With the expansiveness of infinite things,
Like amber, musk, benzoin and incense,
Which sing the raptures of soul and sense.]

The idea of Unity and the synesthesia which proceeds from it are explicitly given in the second quatrain where perfumes, colors and sounds are said to merge into a deep and shadowy oneness like echoes which attenuate into a faraway single sound. The sestet of the poem gives a series of illustrative examples of this merging of sensuous experience. Correspondence is expressed in the comparison of perfume to the tactile smoothness of children's flesh, or to the sweet sound of an oboe, or to the color of green fields. Baudelaire assumed that an infinity of such analogical possibilities was available to the poet.

These same correspondences as well as a number of other important *symboliste* conventions, are to be seen in a second poem by Baudelaire, entitled "Harmonie du Soir." Baudelaire's importance as a pioneer can be understood in the fact that this poem appeared first in *Les Fleurs du Mal* in 1857, nearly thirty years before the hey-day of *symbolisme* in the mid-eighties. As in Verlaine's "Clair de Lune," the poet evokes a strange garden which we come to understand is intimately associated with a beautiful woman and with his own feelings.

Harmonie du Soir

Voici venir les temps où vibrant sur sa tige
Chaque fleur s'évapore ainsi qu'un encensoir;
Les sons et les parfums tournent dans l'air du soir;
Valse mélancolique et langoureux vertige!

Chaque fleur s'évapore ainsi qu'un encensoir;
Le violon frémit comme un coeur qu'on afflige;
Valse mélancolique et langoureux vertige!
Le ciel est triste et beau comme un grand reposoir.

Le violon frémit comme un coeur qu'on afflige,
Un coeur tendre, qui hait le néant vaste et noir!
Le ciel est triste et beau comme un grand reposoir;
Le soleil s'est noyé dans son sang qui se fige.

Un coeur tendre, qui hait le néant vaste et noir,
Du passé lumineux recueille tout vestige!
Le soleil s'est noyé dans son sang qui se fige.
Ton souvenir en moi luit comme un ostensoir.

[Evening Harmony]

[Now comes the time when, vibrating on its stem,
Each flower breathes forth like a censer;
Sounds and perfumes circle in the air of evening;
Melancholy waltz and langorous vertigo!

Each flower breathes forth like a censer;
The violin shudders like a heart that suffers;
Melancholy waltz and languorous vertigo!
The sky, like a great altar, is sad and beautiful.

The violin shudders like a heart that suffers,
A tender heart that hates the vast and dark of Nothingness!
The sky, like a great altar, is sad and beautiful;
The sun is drowning in its own curdled blood.

A tender heart that hates the vast and dark of Nothingness,
Gathers in each vestige of the fading light!
The sun is drowning in its own curdled blood.
Your memory shines in me like a monstrance.]

This poem works by the same indirection which we saw in Verlaine. It is structured as a sequence of declarative statements which seem to focus attention *out there* in the world of phenomena, but which double back at the same time to express some part of the poet's inner world. The violin shuddering like a heart in pain clearly expresses the poet's own feeling; the sun drowning in its own curdled blood suggests the poet's heart drowning in its own despair. The most significant thing is that the poet makes no statement directly about his own heart or about his own feeling; he maintains an apparent objectivity. The first person pronoun appears only in the last line and there in controlled understatement. No gush, no effusion. The poem is about his own despair, about the sensuous beauty of the lost loved one, but these are given only obliquely, that is, *symbolically*, through images of flowers, perfumes, violins, and curdled blood. The images evoke a garden *and* a beautiful woman *and* the poet's despair.

Correspondences are to be seen here, not only between the inner

41

and outer worlds, but also between the various modes of sensuous experience. The motion of the flowers on their stems, the exhalation of their perfume, some unnamed sounds (possibly those of the violin, possibly the remembered sound of a woman's voice), and the lazy vertigo of a waltz all mingle in the evening air to produce a synesthesia of three or four dimensions. Narrative is eschewed in the specific sense, but a whole story is suggested by the last line which implies, but does not state, that the sights and sounds and fragrances of the garden at evening evoke a sacred memory in the poet, but fill him with an overwhelming emptiness, because a love affair once treasured is now over.

This poem illustrates also the radical dependence of the *symboliste* mode upon particular luminous images: flowers that discharge perfumes like censers, violins that throb like hearts in pain, a sky like a great altar, the sun drowning in curdled blood. Placed before the reader without linking commentary, these images comprise almost the entire substance of the poem. As they are used here, they illustrate another common *symboliste* technique—the method of creating a tonality or resonance in a poem by clustering related images, as in the evocation here of an aura of the sacred by repeated reference to censer, altar, and monstrance. A related technique, which was to become equally commonplace in twentieth-century verse, can be seen in the deliberate creation of shock or violent tension by placing the image of curdled blood in the context of evening serenity, or by placing that same image side by side with an object of holy reverence, as in the last two lines. Musicality in this poem can be noted not only in the sonority of the individual lines, but more especially in the incremental repetition of entire lines, which achieve in this fashion the value of motifs.

By a number of these poets themselves, and by some critics since, the *symbolistes* have been called the "*décadents*," and their movement "*décadence*," terms which will be useful for our purpose to designate the attitude toward life which characterized many of these poets. The central part of this attitude was a mood of ennui, the boredom and world-weariness of the man for whom life has no further attractions—neither the pleasures of sense nor of spirit. "*La chair est triste, hélas! et j'ai lu tous les livres,*" ["The flesh is sad, alas! and I have read all the books,"] wrote Mallarmé in an early poem called

"Brise Marine" ["Sea Wind"]. Verlaine exploits this theme in a poem entitled "Langueur" ["Apathy"]. A single voice speaks languidly in the poem, the voice of a Roman who says he is the personification of the Empire at the end of its decadence, watching the tall blond barbarians pass by while he composes idle acrostics in lazy sunlight. The relevance to Verlaine and to his own time and place is transparently clear as the voice says:

L'âme seulette a mal au coeur d'un ennui dense.
Là-bas on dit qu'il est de longs combats sanglants.
O n'y pouvoir, étant si faible aux voeux si lents,
O n'y vouloir fleurir un peu cette existence!

O n'y vouloir, O n'y pouvoir mourir un peu!

[The lonely soul is heartsick from intense boredom.
Over there, they say, is a long, bloody battle.
If only I weren't so feeble with slow desire!
If only I had will to make this life bloom a little!

If only I had the will, the power to die a little!]

Death was the overriding preoccupation of the decadent spirit, the fear of death, fascination and morbid attraction to it, resentment of its inevitable approach, and a conviction that the age itself was permeated by death, that the very century was winding down to an ignominious oblivion. The decadent was typically a man near middle age with a dandy's narcissism and preoccupation with fancy clothing and a contempt for bourgeois proprieties which sometimes led to behavior deliberately intended to shock. In this respect Nerval is often cited, leading a lobster at the end of a long ribbon on the Paris streets, but Nerval had spells of actual insanity and does not provide so good an example as Verlaine and Rimbaud, who conducted a flagrant homosexual affair across France and the low countries, or Baudelaire's excesses with drugs and alcohol, or Mallarmé's counsel and example of withdrawal from active life into the hermetic consolations of art.

All of the *symbolistes*, from Nerval to Mallarmé, felt this alienation from the mass of people. To them poetry was a sacred mystery meant only for the eyes of the initiate and not to be profaned by vulgar eyes. The *symboliste* movement was hermetic not only in its acceptance of occult ideas, but also in its aloofness from the general public and its willingness to foster an esoteric exclusiveness. The difficulty and obscurity of their verse (another of their important bequests to the twentieth century) is a function of this attitude. Having deliberately abandoned many of the conventional literary techniques and traditional symbols of Christian culture, and insisting habitually upon personal and private vision as the authentic source of poetry, they often erected a fabric of personal symbols which was difficult even for an initiate to penetrate.

The decadent sometimes cultivated his esthetic sensibilities to so exquisite a point of refinement that the real world became repellent and real people objects of loathing. An extreme example of such a decadent is Des Esseintes, the central figure of Huysman's novel *A Rebours [Against the Grain,]* who shuns all contact with the outer world and lives like one of Poe's protagonists behind heavy draperies which shut out the daylight. Wealth enables him to satisfy any whim of his hypersensitive taste. He eschews all books except a few Latin poets of Rome's silver decadence and a small number of the contemporary *symbolistes*. He tries to *live* the sensuous correspondences of Baudelaire, playing upon a device which he calls a "mouth organ," a machine which yields a symphony of flavor sensations of cordials and liqueurs. Or he enjoys orgies of sensation based on various scents and perfumes, which he combines like the sounds of music or like lines of poetry. Such sensuous extravaganzas are intended to show Des Esseintes escaping the mundane world of rational consciousness and penetrating into the world of imagination. On one occasion, while never leaving his study, he takes a trip to the seashore by exposing himself to a sequence of the sensations one might have on such a trip: the sight of posters in a railway station, the sound and smell of a locomotive, the smell of salt air and of tarred rope. This would all be a bit absurd if the underlying purpose of the novel were not so serious— to present a detailed program for "blowing the mind," for literally getting out of this world. Schopenhauer had said, "The world is my idea," and these *symbolistes* tried very hard to see how far one could realize this idea in practice. Under strong influence of the French decadents, Oscar Wilde in the late eighties was to develop his hyperbolic paradox that nature, no less than life, is an imitation of art. "For what is Nature?" he demanded. "Nature is no great mother who has borne us. She is our creation. It is in our brain that she quickens to life. Things are because we see them, and what we see and how we see it, depends upon the Arts that have influenced us."[6] In the twentieth century Whitehead was to examine the philosophical implications of this assumption, and Wallace Stevens was to make it a major part of his esthetic creed.

Eroticism is another important part of the decadent attitude and of the *symboliste* poetry, but it is generally a sickly and neurasthenic kind of eros which one encounters there, the perfumed flesh of brothels, or love combined somehow with death, as in the *Liebestod* of Wagner's *Tristan*, or the image of Salomé in seductive jewelled nakedness gazing at the bloody head of John the Baptist as it is brought to her on a charger. Requited love and the consummation of healthy desire are seldom to be found. Much more frequently, withdrawal from the mundane world includes withdrawal from love. Mallarmé's poems sometimes show a more idealized kind of love, but they still reflect a fundamental unwillingness to participate in the blood and mire of physical existence. His famous faun, aroused to lust by the sight of pearly-fleshed nymphs embracing one another in afternoon sleep, is gratified at last by no more than the ironic gesture of blowing upon empty grape skins and by afternoon dreams.

His "Nénuphar Blanc" ["White Water Lily"] shows even more plainly the mistrust of the real world and the insistence upon an idealized world of imagination. The poet, rowing his boat up a quiet stream, comes gently aground upon a clump of reeds. He is in the vicinity of the estate of an unknown lady to whom he is coming to pay respects. He hears what *might* be the rustle of her step on shore behind a hedge. He imagines the perfection of her pure beauty, the white cambric and lace of her skirt, her exquisite sash and diamond buckle. He toys with the thought that all he has to do is to raise his head over the hedge and introduce himself, but he will not break into his dream of the lady, and he rows silently away downstream before she can see him, or anything can happen which will compromise the beauty of his vision. As he goes, he thinks of how he *might* pluck a white, unopened water lily bud to carry away as a remembrance of this moment. But even this objective correlative is only imagined. Nothing happens except his rowing upstream, his pausing, and rowing back down. His hearing of a slight noise, his picture of the lady's beauty, of their encounter, of plucking a white water lily, are all wholly in his imagination. The poem ends with the lines, ". . . And so, like a noble swan's egg, fated never to burst forth in flight, I carried off my imaginary trophy, which bursts only with that exquisite absence of self which many a lady loves to pursue in summer along paths of her park, as she stops sometimes and lingers by a spring which must be crossed or by a lake."—An exquisite piece of writing, shimmering with a beauty which is a limpid stream flowing through green thickets and willow trees softened by silver mist, all of which is a lovely highborn lady, who is a virginal unopened bud of a pure white water lily, which is an unhatched swan's egg, which is the poet's imagination, which is the whole of the poem and of the reality it presents. And we have once more that magic circle which blends subject into object.

As literary movements are wont to do, even one so radically individualistic, *symbolisme* soon produced its own orthodoxy and its own clichés. The noble swan, trapped above in the egg, is one of the most common. He appears again and again, often in a landscape of frozen lakes and glaciers, which themselves become a convention. In Mallarmé's best-known sonnet ("Le vierge, le vivace, et le bel aujourd'hui") the swan is caught in the ice of a frozen lake, his wings fastened immobile, though his head still moves defiantly above the white death. Though he is trapped by his own mortality, and though he is lacerated by the thought that beauty must die and that his own supreme poetic efforts must fail of success, the poet never gives up his disdain of "the soil in which his plumage is trapped." In a few years, nine and fifty such swans will fly up from a chilly lake in one of Yeats' poems.

With all the decadent's pained staring into the mirror of the soul for a glimpse of ineffable beauty or for answers to the questions of being, what he often found instead was the abyss of despair--*le néant, le gouffre, l'abime*. Sometimes this led to Byronic defiance, but more often to the ironic understatement of Laforgue, to the voice which is flippant or deprecates in order to avoid the sob of self-pity or the excess of sentiment which lies just under the surface. His poem "Romance" illustrates the manner, the title intending to lay the ground for bitter irony, the epigraph to evoke the sardonic, brooding version of Shakespeare's Hamlet favored by the *symbolistes*:

Romance
Hamlet: To a nunnery, go

J'ai mille oiseaux de mer d'un gris pâle,
Qui nichent au haut de ma belle âme,
Ils en emplissent les tristes salles
De rythmes pris aux plus fines lames . . .

Or, ils salissent tout de charognes,
Et aussi de coraux, de coquilles;
Puis volent en ronds fous, et se cognent
A mes probes lambris de famille . . .

Oiseaux pâles, oiseaux des sillages!
Quand la fiancée ouvrira la porte,
Faîtes un collier de coquillages
Et que l'odeur de charognes soit forte! . . .

Qu'Elle dise: "Cette âme est bien forte
Pour mon petit nez . . . —je me r'habille.
Mais ce beau collier? hein, je l'emporte?
Il ne lui sert de rien, pauvre fille . . ."

[Romance]
Hamlet: To a nunnery, go

[I have a thousand pale gray sea birds
Which nest high up in my lovely soul,
Whose sad halls they fill
With the set rhythms of the finest waves . . .

Then, they defile all the rotting flesh,
And all the coral and the seashells;
Then fly in mad circles, and knock against
My upright family wainscoting . . .

47

O pale birds, birds with a turbid wake!
When my fiancée opens the door,
Make her a necklace of shellfish
With a good strong odor of carrion . . .

So she will say: "That soul is too strong
For my little nose . . . —I must withdraw.
But that lovely necklace? why not take it along?
It won't do her any good, poor wench . . ."]

The sardonic tone is familiar to twentieth-century English verse
after Pound and Eliot, both of whom had it to an important degree
from Laforgue. The odor of death about the poem is more understandable in Laforgue than in some of the other decadents since for years he
fought off an encroaching turberculosis which at last overwhelmed
him at the early age of twenty-seven. The low view of woman
expressed here passed over without change into such poems as Eliot's
"Prufrock," "Portrait of a Lady," and "The Wasteland." One sees
with particular clarity in this poem the kind of interior "landscape"
which became a major feature of *symboliste* verse. A generation
before Laforgue, Hawthorne and Poe had made extensive use of this
kind of symbolic landscape to express inner psychological states, and
this had been a facet of Poe's writing which particularly engaged
Baudelaire. But the modern English-speaking world learned this
usage not from Poe or Hawthorne, but from Laforgue and his *symboliste* colleagues in Paris.

In a brief account which seeks only to discover the shape of a
particular kind of symbolism, one must forego mention of many
things about this important group of poets. Not that there is a lack of
information about them. An extensive bibliography of writings bears
witness to the endless fascination which they have had for our century.
Poets and critics alike have searched the lives of these poets and their
writings with the passionate concern of men who would discover the
secrets of their own origins, recognizing that with them much of the
modern sensibility first found expression. But this very passion and
the plethora of writings flowing from it are responsible for much of the
confusion which has surrounded "symbolism" as a term in literary
criticism. In these poets we have a widely various and loosely
associated cluster of nineteenth-century French writers who almost by

accident were called *symbolistes*. Because their attitudes and their literary techniques have had profound influence upon twentieth-century literature in all genres, we have used the word "symbolist" to spread over their whole manner and their whole range of techniques, whether all of these had to do specifically with symbolism or not. Laforgue's irony is not in itself symbolic, nor Baudelaire's use of striking images, nor the dandyism, nor the decadent eroticism and preoccupation with death, nor the abandonment of narrative, nor the vogue for the short personal lyric. Yet these poets were true symbolists in a number of ways, beginning with their reverence for the word as Word, as the substance and arm of creativity itself. To them a poem, made of words, lived in both earthly and heavenly realms and thus performed the bridging act of all symbols. It could arouse the soul to contemplation of a beauty above the taint of mutability, and sometimes it could capture and hold glittering particles of that heavenly Beauty itself. These poets were also symbolist in other ways: in their faith that not reason but poetic imagination is man's sovereign gift and that imagination creates the reality men live in; in their attempt to dissolve with words the Cartesian dualism; in their occultism, with its assumption of Unity and its correspondences and synesthesia; in their conception of the poet as magus or seer, whose function is to change the very quality of men's minds and thus their lives; in their appeals to the "soul" through obliquity, indirection, musicality, and metaphoric suggestiveness. The closer one looks, the more he is convinced that in their aims at least they were not so very different from another great poet of symbolism, Dante, whose words described in the waning years of the middle ages another road through the dark hell of human depravity and death up to a celestial rose of heavenly beauty.

Footnotes to Chapter II

[1]There is a substantial bibliography of writings on *Symbolisme*, both on the movement as a whole and on the individual symbolist writers. Useful general introductions to the movement in English are Anna Balakian, *The Symbolist Movement: A Critical Appraisal* (New York, Random House, 1967); René Wellek, *A History of Modern Criticism*, 1750-1950 (New York, 1936), vol. II, *The Romantic Age*; Edmund Wilson, *Axël's Castle* (New York, 1936); Marcel Raymond, *De Baudelaire au Surréalisme* (Paris, 1933) [English

transl.: *From Baudelaire to Surrealism* (New York, 1955)]; C. M. Bowra, *The Heritage of Symbolism* (London, 1943). A volume which had great influence on both Yeats and Eliot is Arthur Symons, *The Symbolist Movement in Literature*, originally published in London, 1899; revised editions, 1908 and 1919; now available in Everyman Paperback. Joseph Chiari, *Symbolisme from Poe to Mallarmé* (London, 1956) and Angelo Bertocci, *From Symbolism to Baudelaire* (Carbondale, 1964) give extensive discussions of the metaphysical backgrounds of the movement. One of the most fascinating studies of the movement, a book containing highly suggestive material for the study of other nineteenth and twentieth-century authors, is John Senior, *The Way Down and Out; the Occult in Symbolist Literature* (Ithaca, N.Y., 1959). All of the above contain select bibliographies, the most useful of which are Balakian, Bertocci, and Senior. A. G. Lehmann, *The Symbolist Aesthetic in France 1885-1895* (Oxford, Basil Blackwell, 1950) gives an exhaustive treatment of theoretical backgrounds to the movement. The French symbolist poets have been frequently translated in recent years. For a generous anthology in paperback by a number of translators, see Angel Flores, ed. *An Anthology of French Poetry from Nerval to Valéry* (New York, 1958). C. F. MacIntyre has translated a number of these poets including Baudelaire, *One Hundred Poems from Les Fleurs Du Mal* (Berkeley, 1947); Corbiere, *Selections from Les Amours Jaunes* (Berkeley, 1954); Mallarmé, *Selected Poems* (Berkeley, 1957); Verlaine, *Selected Poems* (Berkeley, 1948). A paperback selection of forty poems by eight *symboliste* poets, from Nerval to Valéry, by the same translator is *French Symbolist Poetry* (Berkeley, 1958).

[2]Of Poe's esthetic doctrines, the following were of greatest importance to the *symbolistes*: (1) that beauty is the chief province of poetry, a beauty which is known by a certain "elevation of the soul"; (2) that poetry should be "pure," untainted by didacticism or concern for the mundane; (3) that there is no such thing as a long poem; (4) that indefiniteness and indirection are the best means of evoking poetic Beauty; (5) that rhythmic and musical devices are among the most powerful poetic means. A number of other specifics from Poe's career fround their way into *symboliste* theory or practice: the career which combined the activities of both poet and critic; the stance of alienation from a callous or hostile society (Baudelaire described Poe as a virtual martyr of philistine society); the obsession with darkness and death; the stress upon imagination and the distrust of reason; the occultism. In a word, one can find in Poe the basis for the entire *symboliste* program.

[3]Stéphane Mallarmé. "The Evolution of Literature," in *Selected Prose, Poems, Essays, and Letters*, ed. and transl. by Bradford Cook (Baltimore, 1856), p. 21.

[4]All translations herein are my own. They stress the literal.

[5]*Aurélia*, in *Oeuvres*, ed. Albert Béguin and Jean Richer (Paris, 1952-1956), I, 403.

[6]Quoted in Richard Ellmann and Charles Feidelson Jr., *The Modern Tradition: Backgrounds of Modern Literature* (New York, 1965), p. 21.

CHAPTER THREE

The Dream Symbolism of Freud and Jung

When Jesus was brought before the Procurator of Judea for judgment, one part of the "evidence" which Pilate took into consideration was a plea from his own wife to let this man go free, because she had suffered terribly the night before from a dream about him. Her plea was not enough to stiffen Pilate's impulse to set Jesus free, but the dream was thought important enough by the evangelist to be recorded in the brief gospel account, and the incident joins many others in which dreams are central to the events recorded in scripture—Jacob and the vision of the celestial stairway; Joseph interpreting the Pharaoh's dream of seven fat cows and seven lean; Ezekiel and the vision of the fiery wheel in the sky; John and the elaborate vision of the apocalypse.

Freud mentions in the opening paragraph of his book *On Dreams* (1901) the universal interest of the pre-scientific ages in dreams, which were looked upon as a means of reading the influence of higher powers, demonic or divine, upon human life; and he noted that when scientific modes of thought became dominant, "all this ingenuous mythology was transformed into psychology." Not quite all, perhaps, for one can still buy dream books or almanacs at any newsstand containing elaborate listings of dream symbols and their meaning. But for most of the modern Western World, the only way in which the symbolism of dreams has been respectable in recent years is as a phase of depth psychology. This symbolism exists in two major modes, the

52

Freudian and the Jungian, which are distinct from one another, though Jung was one of Freud's close associates for a number of years. Partly because of the great prestige of Freud's techniques of psychoanalysis, his theory of symbolism has been widely known for an entire generation, even among laymen, and has exercised a major influence on the literature of our century. The least sophisticated among us know that all sharp-pointed objects are to be regarded as symbolic of the phallus, and that all hollow or enclosing objects are to be regarded as symbolic of the vagina; that inadvertencies of speech are "Freudian slips," symbolic of our deepest unspoken desires and ideas. Jung's theory of symbols, a much more elaborate structure developed from a base in Freud, has caught public imagination more slowly, though his ideas begin to be reflected in literature and criticism in recent years with increasing frequency. The two systems are best distinguished by their assumptions about the nature of the unconscious. Because Freud was the pioneer, it is appropriate to describe his system first, and to get at his idea of symbol, it is necessary to discuss his theory of dreams.[1]

I

Freud's interest in symbols had its origin in his study of neurotic patients. He noted that the physical symptoms of neurosis were at times symbolic: a patient might develop asthma because "he couldn't breathe the atmosphere at home"; another might vomit because of a situation which "he could not stomach," or develop spasms over something "he could not swallow." Such neurosis, he assumed, was only one way in which submerged parts of the psyche found expression; dreams were another way. This meant that dreams were also related to parts of earlier conscious experience and that their symbolic content might thus provide a means of access to the causes of neurosis. He developed a technique of "free association" for connecting the symbols in dreams with the parts of the consciousness which were their causes.

The first full statement of his theory of symbolism was given in *The Interpretation of Dreams* (1900), followed the next year by a little book, *On Dreams*, which stated his ideas in synoptic form. He assumes that the human psyche is made up of two parts, the consciousness and the unconscious, and that between these two in a kind of frontier zone exists an arbiter which he called the Censor. This Censor passes judgment on those portions of the unconscious—desires, drives, thoughts, instinctual urges—which seek conscious expression. Those which are agreeable, it passes; those which are not it represses. The driving force of the psyche, its fountain of psychic energy, Freud called the libido, which he thought to be chiefly sexual in nature. He assumed that all human beings as children have extensive sexual drives, which are largely repressed, the Oedipal urge, for example, and that these repressed infantile sexual drives are of the greatest importance in the psychic life of adults.

When some urge or idea is rejected by the Censor, it does not leave the psyche, but drops back into the unconscious where it retains its charge of psychic energy and continues to seek conscious expression, often by losing its literal form and assuming symbolic form. Under some conditions, most notably in sleep, the Censor is relaxed, so that it is possible for what has been repressed to find its way to consciousness. But since the censorship is never completely removed, but only reduced, repressed material must undergo a change, often a radical conversion of its more offensive features, before it can find expression. For this reason, a large part of psychic activity during the dream state is essentially, in Freud's view, a symbolic process in which the dream substitutes acceptable content for that which has been rejected.

He distinguishes between the "manifest content" of a dream, the actual events or images or feelings of the dream itself, and the "latent content," which is not what is experienced in the dream, but consists of things which prompted the dream, events of the previous day, sensory impressions during sleep, and the like. One discovers this latent content by the key technique of "analysis" in which one divides a dream into component parts, contemplates each part separately, and records whatever thoughts or impressions arise to mind during this process of free association.

An example should make this clearer. In *The Interpretation of Dreams* Freud records the following dream by a woman patient (This is the dream's manifest content): "The dreamer sees three lions in a desert, one of which is laughing, but she is not afraid of them. Then, however, she must have fled from them for she is trying to climb a tree, but she finds that her cousin, who is a teacher of French, is already up in the tree, etc." Now the dream's latent content is discovered by "analysis"; the woman is questioned next day about separate parts of the dream, and the following associations are recorded:

A sentence in the dreamer's English lesson had become the indifferent occasion for it (the dream): "The *lion's* greatest beauty is his mane." Her father wore a beard which surrounded his face like a mane. The name of her English teacher was Miss *Lyons*. An acquaintance of hers had sent her the ballads of Loewe (German, Loewe—lion). These, then, are the three lions; why should she have been afraid of them? She has read a story in which a negro who has incited his fellows to revolt is hunted with bloodhounds and climbs a tree to save himself. Then follows fragments in a wanton mood, like the following. Directions for catching lions from *Die Fliegende Blaetter*: "Take a desert and strain it; the lions will remain." Also an amusing, but not very proper anecdote about an official who is asked why he does not take greater pains to win the favor of his superior officer, and who answers that he has been trying to insinuate himself, but that the man ahead of him *is already up*. The whole matter becomes intelligible as soon as one learns that on the day of the dream the lady had received a visit from her husband's superior. He was very polite to her, kissed her hand, and *she was not afraid of him at all*, although he is a "big bug" (German—Grosses Tier—"big animal") and plays the part of a "social lion."[2]

Several parts of "dream work," the processes through which latent content is converted into the manifest content, can be seen in the above: first of all, the manner in which dream thoughts are expressed dramatically, in *visual images* resembling the metaphors of poetic discourse. In her dream, the woman has an experience, not of thinking thoughts, but of participating in a sequence of actions, absurd though they may appear next day to the conscious mind. Second, the principle of *condensation*, whereby a dream makes a composite or conflation of apparently disparate elements which must nevertheless have some element in common. Here the sentence from the woman's English lesson, her father's mane-like beard, and a joke from a magazine are reduced to three lions in the desert, one of whom is laughing. Third, the great importance to dream work of *word meanings*, particularly of verbal ambiguities, such as the ribald word-play involved in the story of the man who was "already up," the poet Loewe depicted in the dream as "lion," and the pun involving *grosses Tier* and "social lion."

A fourth major part of dream work, not obvious in this example, Freud called *displacement,* one of the chief ways in which a dream disguises its material so as to pass the Censor. This refers to a displacement of emphasis or psychic energy from what is truly essential or important in the dream to something trivial, so that what is recalled of the dream with greatest clarity and distinctness consists of insignificant details, while the central substance of the dream is recalled only in blurred or indistinct fashion.

Freud assumed that virtually all dreams are prompted by egoistic factors, particularly the fulfillment of erotic desire. He divided dreams into three categories: (1) intelligible dreams, which are almost invariably undisguised wish-fulfillments (Most dreams of children are of this kind); (2) dreams expressing disguised wish-fulfillment (the overwhelming majority of adult dreams are of this sort, and largely of erotic content); (3) dreams presenting repressed desires without disguise (and therefore accompanied by strong feelings of anxiety). He insisted upon the primacy of erotic substance in the dreams of adults because, "no other impulse has had to undergo such suppression from the time of childhood as the sex impulse in its numerous components; from no other impulse have survived so many and such intense unconscious wishes . . ." *(Interpretation*, p. 240)

The manner in which a dream converts repressed erotic material into more acceptable symbolic form can be illustrated by the following: "The dreamer relates: Between two stately palaces stands a little house, receding somewhat, whose doors are closed. My wife leads me a little way along the street up to the little house, and pushes in the door, and then I slip quickly and easily into the interior of a courtyard that slants obliquely upward." This seems innocuous enough for a dream, but here is how Freud translates its true "meaning":

Anyone who has had experience in the translating of dreams will, of course, immediately perceive that penetrating into narrow spaces, and opening locked doors belong to the commonest sexual symbolism, and will easily find in this dream a represen-

56

tation of attempted coition from behind (between the two stately buttocks of the female body). The narrow slanting passage is of course the vagina; the assistance attributed to the wife of the dreamer requires the interpretation that in reality it is only consideration for the wife which is responsible for the detention from such an attempt. Moreover, inquiry shows that on the previous day a young girl had entered the household of the dreamer who had pleased him, and who had given him the impression that she would not be altogether opposed to an approach of this sort. The little house between the two palaces is taken from a reminiscence of the Hradschin in Prague, and thus points again to the girl who is a native of that city. (*Interpretation*, pp. 241-242)

Freud warned against repeating the error of the dream books by interpreting dream symbolism in too mechanical a fashion. He urged the interpreter to keep in mind the curious plasticity of psychic material and the unpredictability of the symbolizing process, but in spite of such warnings he himself was willing to make long lists of dream symbols like the following:

Emperor and Empress (King and Queen) in most cases really represent the parents of the dreamer; the dreamer himself or herself is the prince or princess. All elongated objects, sticks, tree-trunks, and umbrellas (on account of the stretching-up which might be compared to an erection!) all elongated and sharp weapons, knives, daggers, and pikes, are intended to represent the male member. A frequent, not very intelligible symbol for the same is a nailfile (on account of the rubbing and scraping?). Little cases, boxes, caskets, closets, and stoves correspond to the female part . . . The dream of walking through a row of rooms is a brothel or harem dream. Staircases, ladders, and flights of stairs, or climbing on these either upwards or downwards, are symbolic representations of the sexual act. Smooth walls over which one is climbing, facades of houses upon which one is letting oneself down, frequently under great anxiety, correspond to the erect human body, and probably repeat in the dream reminiscences of the upward climbing of little children on their parents or foster parents. Smooth walls are men . . . Tables, set

57

tables, and boards are women, perhaps on account of the opposition which does away with the bodily contours . . . Of articles of dress the woman's hat may frequently be definitely interpreted as the male genital. In dreams of men one often finds the cravat as a symbol for the penis . . . All complicated machines and apparatus in dreams are very probably genitals, in the description of which dream symbolism shows itself to be as tireless as the activity of wit. Likewise many landscapes in dreams, especially with bridges or wooded mountains, can be readily recognized as descriptions of the genitals. (*Interpretation*, pp. 246-247.)

Freud's followers carried lists of this kind much further, and in spite of all the disclaimers, one cannot escape the impression that an orthodoxy of symbols and standardized meanings came to be established, and that both Freud and his disciples sometimes read dreams in reductive and simplistic fashion. The following is a dream interpretation given in the third edition of *The Interpretation of Dreams*:

Then someone broke into the house and anxiously called for a policeman. But he went with two tramps by mutual consent into a church, (Or chapel—vagina) to which led a great many stairs (symbol of coitus); behind the church there was a mountain (Mons veneris), on top of which is a dense forest (Crines pubis). The policeman was furnished with a helmet, a gorget, and a cloak (Demons in cloaks and capucines, are, according to the explanation of a man versed in the subject, of a phallic nature.). The two vagrants, who went along with the policeman quite peaceably, had tied to their loins sack-like aprons (The two halves of the scrotum). A road led from the church to the mountain. This road was overgrown on each side with grass and brushwood, which becomes thicker and thicker as it reaches the height of the mountain, where it spread out into quite a forest.

An interpretation of this kind is something like the common form of allegory in which a set of pictorial images exists in a one-to-one relationship with a set of abstract equivalents.[3] The dream symbols such as the policeman above, the two tramps, the church, the forest, are looked upon as signs pointing to previous experience and to sexual equivalents in the *a priori* scheme of psychoanalysis. The interpreter is less interested in the symbols themselves than in what they point to; they have chiefly a communicative function.

Underneath the Freudian symbol theory, one notes the strong presence of basic attitudes of nineteenth-century empirical science. The symbol system is conceived within a frame of physical or biological existence and is related to pathology of individuals. While it is concerned with emotional or psychic factors, it approaches these analytically with the intention of placing them under rational control. In this context there is no religious dimension to life and no transcendence.

As we have said, Freud clearly recognized that the symbolism in dreams was not peculiar to dreams, but seemed to be a fundamental characteristic of the unconscious itself, and would therefore be manifested wherever the unconscious found conscious expression. "Dream symbolism extends far beyond dreams," he wrote, "it is not peculiar to dream, but exercises a similar dominating influence on representation in fairy tales, myths and legends, in jokes and folklore. It enables us to trace the intimate connections between dreams and these latter productions. We must not suppose that dream symbolism is a creation of the dream work; it is in all probability a characteristic of the unconscious thinking which provides the dream work with the material for condensation, displacement, and dramatization."[4] C.G. Jung was to examine in great detail the connections between dream symbolism and the symbolism of folk-expression, art, and literature, and we can turn now to his system.

II

Jung assumed like Freud that the unconscious part of the psyche manifests itself in symbols, and most commonly in dreams, but he evolved a somewhat different conception of the unconscious and a much more elaborate theory of symbolism. He extended Freud's two "levels" of the psyche to three: the consciousness, the personal unconscious, and the collective unconscious. Whereas Freud had assumed a state of continuous conflict between the consciousness, which was seen as good, and the unconscious, which was seen as bad, Jung thought of the psyche as unitary, full of all manner of things, to be sure, dark and light, evil and good, rational and irrational, but of positive connotation overall, because in his view the three levels were one and constituted the dynamic guiding principle of growth and development within a man. He accepted the Freudian principle of repression, but he thought that Freud's conception of the unconscious as a kind of dumping-ground for the rejected past was too limited.

Such repressed material constituted only part of the unconscious. In Jung's view, the subliminal material of the unconscious consisted not only of "all urges, impulses and intentions; all perceptions and intuitions; all rational or irrational thoughts, conclusions, inductions, deductions, and premises; and all varieties of feeling,"[5] but also of *totally new contents, never yet a part of consciousness, which could be produced spontaneously by the unconscious itself.* This last hypothesis, that the unconscious produces its own fruitful germs of future psychic events, represents a major departure from Freud and a pivotal concept in Jung's entire psychological system.

Freud had thought the libido to be mainly sexual, but Jung saw it much more broadly as "psychic energy." He retained, like Freud, a lifelong commitment to clinical psychiatric practice, but his theory of symbols went far beyond the pathology of individuals to include extensions into a wide spectrum of cultural and social areas—religion, anthropology, literature and the arts, history and sociology. In promulgating his ideas, he drew not only upon Western science, philosophy, theology, and literature, but upon a number of the great oriental religions and upon alchemy and other occult systems as well. Much of his enlarged view of the symbol is developed from his theories of the "collective unconscious" and the "archetypes," unfortunate terms which he spent much of his later life trying to clarify for a world which insisted on misreading them.

Following Freud's hypothesis, Jung assumed that the psyche, like man's physical body, is a product of an evolutionary process extending far back into primordial antiquity, and that consciousness is a late acquisition of man, a thin veneer on the surface of an unconscious which is unimaginably ancient and vast, a spaceless space within as infinite in its dimension and potential as the cosmos outside man. This contains not only a dimension of personal psychic material peculiar to the individual—his repressed desires and the like—but also a much larger dimension of the collective unconscious which is generic to man's psychic being in the same fashion that his body is generic to man's physical being. The collective unconscious is made up of the archetypes.

The archetypes are not images or representations or ideas, but are tendencies, channels, or predispositions. They are not precisely instincts (though they are instinctual), but are inherited *modes* of psychic function corresponding to the inborn tendency of a chick to hatch from an egg, or the tendency of a bird to build its nest. Jung first called them the "dominants" of the collective unconscious. As constituent parts of the mysterious depths of the psyche, they are in themselves unknowable, and can be known to consciousness only indirectly through images which they project and which symbolically represent the nature and content of a particular archetype. It is these symbols, produced *spontaneously* by the archetypes within the collective unconscious, and known principally in dreams, which are man's chief contact with the primordial depths of his psyche. Within every modern man dwells something of all the earlier psychic experience of the race, but Jung assumed that, far from being a dead deposit, this is a *living* system of tendencies and formative principles which function more or less the same in all of us and determine the very nature of human life.

The archetypes bid fair to remain sufficiently mysterious, because there is a marked reluctance on the part of everyone, including Jung and his disciples, to make any listing of them. One can compile a list of the archetypes about which Jung himself has written most frequently something as follows: The Magna Mater or World Mother, the Great Father, the Miraculous Child, the Hero, the Rebirth of the Hero, the World Tree, the Trickster, the Wise Old Man, the Descent into Hell, the Earthly Paradise or Golden Age. To this list one should add several aspects of the psyche which Jung saw as archetypal: The Anima, the Animus, the Shadow, the Persona, the process of Individuation. Philip Wheelwright has made a somewhat different listing of the archetypes as follows: the Divine Father, the Earth Mother, the World Tree, the Satyr or Centaur or other man-animal monster, the Descent into Hell, the Purgatorial Stair, the washing away of sin, the castle of attainment, the culture-hero such as Prometheus bringing fire or other basic gifts to mankind, the sacrificial death of the god, the god in disguise or the prince under an enchantment. . . ."[6] Because the archetypes are assumed to have both an individual and a collective (i.e. racial or cultural) expression, they have been invoked in literary criticism as a means of studying not only poetry itself but also the poet's unconscious and his inherited cultural patterns. For our purpose here in describing symbol-theory it is most useful to think of the archetypes simply as tendencies, the shaping source of all the symbols which arise from the collective unconscious.

A more concrete idea of the archetypes can be obtained from one of Jung's own dream analyses, which was recorded in the first chapter of his book *Modern Man in Search of a Soul*, (1933). He had been called in as a psychiatric consultant in the case of a young girl who was having symptoms of hysteria and the beginning of a progressive atrophy of the muscles. When he asked her in the course of treatment about her dreams, she related two recent dreams of terrifying nature. In the first of these she saw her mother hanging by the neck from a chandelier and swinging to and fro in a cold wind; in the second she saw a frightened horse crashing about frantically through the upper rooms of her house and eventually jumping from an open window to land in a mangled heap on the street four floors below.

Jung does not resort in his reading of these two dreams to Freud's "analysis," that process of free-association intended to discover what previous conscious experience has been repressed and is now finding symbolic expression in dreams. Instead, he assumes that the two major events in these dreams are symbols expressive of archetypes from the collective unconscious, that they have *spontaneously* arisen within the dream, and that they have to do as much with future potential for the dreamer as with anything from the past. Because he assumes that the archetypes find expression in a wide variety of media such as folklore, myth, art, and literature, he resorts to material of this kind as a means of interpreting these dreams. It is necessary to quote extensively in order to represent his method fairly:

> The way in which these dreams allude to death is enough to give one pause. But many persons have anxiety dreams now and then. We must therefore look more closely into the meaning of the outstanding symbols, "mother" and "horse." These figures must be equivalent one to the other, for they both do the same thing: they commit suicide. The mother symbol is archetypal and refers to a place of origin, to nature, the lower body (womb) and the vegetative functions. It connotes also the unconscious,

natural and instinctive life, the physiological realm, the body in which we dwell or are contained, for the 'Mother' is also a vessel, the hollow form (*uterus*) that carries and nourishes, and it thus stands for the foundations of consciousness. Being within something or contained in something suggests darkness, the nocturnal—a state of anxiety. With these allusions I am presenting the idea of the mother in many of its mythological and etymological transformations; I am also giving an important part of the *yin* concept of Chinese philosophy. All this is a dream-content, but it is not something which the seventeen-year-old girl has acquired in her individual existence; it is rather a bequest from the past [that is, from the *collective unconscious*]. On the one hand it has been kept alive by the language, and on the other hand it is inherited with the structure of the psyche and is therefore to be found in all times and among all peoples.

The familiar word "mother" refers apparently to the best-known of mothers in particular—to "my mother." But the mother symbol (as in the dream) points to a darker meaning which eludes conceptual formulation and can only be vaguely apprehended as the hidden, nature-bound life of the body. Yet even this expression is too narrow, and excludes too many pertinent side-meanings. The psychic reality which underlies this symbol [i.e. the archetype], is so inconceivably complex that we can only discern it from afar off, and then but very dimly, it is such realities that call for symbolic expression.[7]

So the archetype is not the actual symbol; it is the node of energy and the formative principle underlying and sending up the symbol from the collective unconscious. Expressions of the mother-archetype will have a generic similarity wherever they appear in the literature, art, or mythology of widely differing peoples and cultures, or in the dreams of individuals. But they will not be identical and they will not be "inherited images," as the archetypes have sometimes been called. It is worth noting that for Jung the archetypes, like all other aspects of psychic reality, involve the idea of antithetical opposites in antagonistic relationship, so that the mother-archtype includes images of tender care and mother love and, at the same time, of the terrible or devouring mother, the principle of death and destruction. This clash of dialectical opposites is one reason why the archetypes lie forever beyond the grasp of conscious reason with its demand for logical consistency.

Jung's comments on the horse symbol in the second dream illustrate once more the essential mystery of the archetypes and his recourse to folk-materials as means of interpreting the symbols expressive of the archetypes:

> "Horse" is an archetype that is widely current in mythology and folklore. As an animal it represents the non-human psyche, the sub-human, animal side, and therefore the unconscious. This is why the horse in folklore sometimes sees visions, hears voices, and speaks. As a beast of burden it is closely related to the mother-archetype: the Valkyries bear the dead hero to Valhalla and the Trojan horse encloses the Greeks. As an animal lower than man, it represents the lower part of the body and the animal drives that take their rise from there. The horse is dynamic power and a means of locomotion; it carries one away like a surge of instinct. It is subject to panics like all instinctive creatures who lack higher consciousness. Also it has to do with sorcery and magical spells—especially the black, night horse which heralds death.
>
> It is evident, then that "horse" is the equivalent of "mother" with a slight shift of meaning. The mother stands for life at its origin, and the horse for the merely animal life of the body. If we apply this meaning to the dream, it says: the animal life destroys itself.
>
> The two dreams make nearly the same assertion, but, as is usually the case, the second is more specific. The peculiar subtlety of the dream is brought out in both instances: there is no mention of the death of the individual. It is notorious that one often dreams of one's own death, but that is no serious matter. When it is really a question of death the dream speaks another language. Both of these dreams, then, point to a serious and even fatal, organic disease. The prognosis was shortly after borne out in fact.

This reads a bit like modern sooth-saying, but it was Jung's conviction, and that of his followers, that such archetypal symbols, sent up from the unconscious, do indeed embody the open future, as a seed embodies the future oak tree. The symbol need not be of a future catastrophe; it could just as well be herald of a stage of growth. The unconscious, even though it contains material of every sort, light and dark, silly and sublime, is *neutral* in characteristic for Jung, achieving moral value only when objectified in human experience. Freud's model of the psyche tended toward stasis or equilibrium, but for Jung the keynote of the psyche is growth, and the symbols which relate to it are therefore to be conceived of, not as fixed, but as moving expressions of archetypes which are also moving and forever changing in aspect. This conviction that symbols embody the future is one side of Jung's symbol theory which borders upon the occult, for he thought of the archetypes as part of the ineffable substance of divine creativity itself, and of the archetypal symbols as the conscious mind's chief access to the mystery of the divine. To be open and receptive to symbolic suggestiveness, then, is to have insight like that of a mystic or a religious seer.

The question naturally arises, how does one know whether he is dealing with a "big" dream or a "little" one, with an archetypal symbol or with some dream-echo of personal experience? The answer which Jung gives is that archetypal symbols are "numinous," that is, highly charged with psychic energy. When one of these passes over into consciousness, it is felt as an illumination, a revelation or saving idea, which carries a summons to action, a stimulus which arouses the whole being to a total reaction; one knows an archetypal symbol because he is seized and compelled by it.

One of Jung's followers, Gerhard Adler, describes true symbols as "irritants" to the conscious mind: "Symbols represent psychic contents that cannot be expressed in any other form," he wrote. "Any true symbol is bound to contain an irrational (nonrational) element: an element that eludes conscious definition. In this way the symbol irritates the conscious mind into attempting to understand and formulate its meaning by a continuous process of circumambulation and approximation. Symbols have thus a peculiar fascination for and a dynamic effect on the conscious mind, 'provoking' it to integrate them into consciousness. They provide a stimulus for contemplation by which more and more contents of the unconscious, condensed in symbolic images, are forced into consciousness."[8]

It can be seen that in Jungian dream-interpretation perhaps even more than in Freudian, the role of the interpreter is of great importance, for here, since the symbol is assumed by definition to have a variable, mysterious, and indefinite character, its meaning will be available only in proportion to the expertise, the learning, and the intuitive perception of the one who reads it. The more exhaustive his knowledge of the archetypes and of their expressions in myth and folklore, the more he will be able to perceive of a dream-symbol's implied meanings. Jung steadfastly refused to formulate a general theory of dream interpretation, but insisted that each approach to interpretation should be tentative and flexible, and should be shaped to the particular religious, philosophical, and existential background of the individual subject. He recognized the existence of certain relatively fixed dream motifs, such as falling, flying, being pursued by dangerous animals, being insufficiently clothed in a public place, but he insisted that even these had an indefinite content which distinguished them from signs. He criticized Freudian theory and practice as too restrictive because it tended to see most dream-symbols as fixed signs or as symptoms of events external to the psyche.

"I prefer to regard the symbol," he wrote, "as the announcement of something unknown, hard to recognize, and not to be fully determined. Take for instance the so-called phallic symbols, which are supposed to stand for the *membrum virile* and nothing more. Psychologically speaking, the *membrum* is itself . . . a symbolic image whose wider content cannot easily be determined. . . . Its equivalents in mythology and in dreams are the bull, the ass, the pomegranate, the yoni, the he-goat, the lightning, the horse's hoof, the dance, the magical cohabitation in the furrow, and the menstrual fluid, to mention only a few of many. That which underlies all of these images—and sexuality itself—is an archetypal content that is hard to grasp, and that finds its best psychological expression in the primitive *mana* symbol."[9]

He himself made careful distinction between sign and symbol. Much of language he thought to have a sign or semiotic function because words are commonly used as means of communicating known meanings. Other common objects have sign functions, such as a policeman's badge, a soldier's insignia, or designs used as trade marks. "A word is *symbolic*," he wrote, "when it implies something more than its obvious and immediate meaning. It has a wider 'unconscious' aspect that can never be precisely explained. Nor can one hope to define or explain it. As the mind explores the symbol, it is led to ideas that lie beyond the grasp of reason.''[10] A true symbol is ''living'' because it is pregnant with meaning. It can never be consciously made from known materials, but can only be discovered or experienced. Once the meaning has been born out of it, once it has been rationalized, it becomes a conventional sign. The same object may be a symbol or a sign depending upon who contemplates it, as the cross to a devout Catholic may radiate complex and compelling symbolic meanings, while to an unbeliever it may have only sign value as an emblem designating the Christian religion.

Since symbols were for Jung the chief means of bridging the conscious and unconscious portions of the psyche, they are understandably important to many facets of his psychological theory, including the central concept of Individuation. He conceived of the psyche as a self-regulating system whose health depends upon an equilibrium of opposing qualities. Individuation is the process of achieving wholeness, of realizing one's own truest Self, a process in which a number of these opposing aspects of the psyche must be brought into balance. Within each man, for example, as a counterpart to the positive Ego, there exists a dark side of the personality, the collocation of all one's negative characteristics, to which Jung gave the name of the Shadow. This he thought to be symbolized often in dreams as a man with ferocious or bestial qualities or in literature by such figures as Shakespeare's Caliban or by the Mr. Hyde of Stevenson's famous story. Another dimension of the psyche he called the Anima, which he conceived of as the inner female counterpart to a man's maleness. The Anima is symbolized in dreams by a variety of female figures, some with an aura of divinity like the Virgin Mary; some of sinister or demonic aspect like a witch or siren; some erotic, like the beautiful princess in the opera *Turandot* who requires suitors to answer enigmatic riddles or forfeit their lives. In corresponding fashion, Jung taught that women have an inner male counterpart, which he called the Animus, and which he said has a similar scale of symbolic possibilities in dreams, ranging from a threatening or sinister figure like Blue-beard, to a person of erotic physical appeal like Tarzan, or a chivalric knight like Gawain or Launcelot. Still another dimension of the psyche he called the Persona or Mask, which he

67

thought of as a composite of the qualities making up the public personality, the face which one turns toward the world. The Persona he thought to be symbolized in dreams as a cloak or coat.

Jung was particularly interested in the *mandala* which he saw as the symbol of psychic wholeness or achieved Individuation. The mandala is a symbolic design, often in the form of a flower or a wheel, in which the design elements are arranged so as to express both a circle and a square which are intimately related around a center of high significance. Versions of the mandala are found among all peoples and cultures from paleolithic times to the present, among the most sophisticated as among the most primitive. The great rose windows of the Gothic churches are examples of the mandala, as is the rose in the final portions of Dante's *Paradiso. Yantras*, those symbolic designs used by oriental occultists to assist the process of meditation, are other examples of mandalas. Such designs often appeared spontaneously in the dreams of Jung's patients, and he thought of them as archetypal and expressive of the wholeness resulting from the harmonizing or unifying of conflicting elements within the psyche.

Jung's symbol theory had important collective or social aspects as well as relevance to individuals. He was convinced that modern Western man is involved in a major crisis involving symbols, that he suffers from a neurosis in which the consciousness has become dangerously dissociated from its nourishing substratum of the unconscious. Primitive man, because his psychic life was comprised much more largely of unconscious factors, felt an emotional oneness with nature, but too great an emphasis upon rational consciousness has deprived modern man of this identity with phenomena and of his capacity to respond to numinous symbols, with the result that he feels isolated in the cosmos. This holds true at the individual level (Jung claimed that two-thirds of his mental patients suffered from nothing more than this sense of helplessness and isolation and futility), and at the collective level as well. The crisis in religious faith, the two World Wars, and the general social unrest of modern times he saw as signs of a serious psychic split. Jung was convinced that the dominating symbols of Western culture are progressively losing their power to compel men's actions, and that therefore the institutions based upon them are crumbling away. In this fashion Western man finds himself impoverished both of fructifying numinous symbols from the uncon-

68

scious and of the cultural symbols which bind together and motivate society.

Psychic health can be restored, he thought, only if we develop the imaginative and emotional openness to understand once more the forgotten language of the unconscious, through sympathetic study of myths, literature, and the arts, but most of all through learning to read the symbols in dreams. The present world crisis shows that we need new and viable symbols to recharge our lives with meaning, but these will be manifested only to receptive individuals. Wholeness can come only from within.

Footnotes to Chapter III

[1]Both Freud and Jung were prolific writers, and both were blessed with numerous disciples who were also prolific writers. References to symbolism occur throughout their basic writings, but Freud's own most completely developed discussion of symbolism is to be found in *The Interpretation of Dreams* (1900), rev. 1908, 1913, 1932, etc.; in *On Dreams* (1901); and in *New Introductory Lectures On Psychoanalysis* (1916-1917), esp. Lectures 1-11. An early commentary on Freud's theory of symbolism is by his well-known British disciple, Ernest Jones, "The Theory of Symbolism," *British Journal of Psychology*, IX (1918), 181 f. A useful general introduction to psychoanalytic theory, including the theory of symbolism, is Patrick Mullahy, *Oedipus: Myth and Complex; A Review of Psychoanalytic Theory* (New York, 1948). Two books by Wilhelm Stekel, *Die Sprache des Traumes* (Wiesbaden, 1911), and *The Interpretation of Dreams: New Developments and Techniques*, transl. by Eden and Cedar Paul (New York, 1943), are extensions of Freud's approach to dream symbolism by a brilliant disciple, who goes much further than Freud in the direction of symbol catalogs. Roy P. Basler's *Sex, Symbolism, and Psychology* (New Brunswick, N.J., 1948) is based on Freudian theory, and gives readings of a number of poems and short stories, but contains very little of the theory of symbolism or of psychology. Frederick J. Hoffman's *Freudianism and the Literary Mind* (Baton Rouge, La., 1945) contains a sound digest of Freudian ideas, including a brief treatment of his theory of symbolism, an account of the growth of Freud's

influence on literature, and essays on the Freudian dimension of such writers as D. H. Lawrence, Waldo Frank, Kafka, and Thomas Mann. *Organization and Pathology of Thought*, ed. David Rapaport (New York, 1951), Part III, "Symbolism," contains essays on symbolism by a number of psychologists.

Particularly useful for Jung's theory of symbolism is Jolande Jacobi, *Complex/Archetype/Symbol in the Psychology of C. G. Jung*, transl. by Ralph Manheim (New York, 1959), a compilation of Jung's important statements on these three concepts, with a running interpretive commentary; and by the same author, *The Psychology of C. G. Jung: An Introduction with Illustrations*, transl. K. W. Bash (London, 1942). *Man and His Symbols*, ed. by C. G. Jung (New York, Dell, 1968), contains a 100-page popular introduction to his psychology by Jung himself, and essays by several of his closest associates, M-L. von Franz, Joseph L. Henderson, Jolande Jacobi, Aniela Jaffe. Jung's earlier collection of essays, *Modern Man in Search of a Soul*, transl. by W. S. Dell and Cary F. Barnes (New York, 1933), now available in paperback, (New York, Harvest books, 1963), contains important material on symbolism. See esp. chapters 1, 6, 7, 10. Two books by Ira Progoff are valuable: *Jung's Psychology and Its Social Meaning* (New York, 1953); and *The Symbolic and the Real* (New York, 1963). Erich Neumann makes dramatic use of Jung's theory of symbolism in *The Origins and History of Consciousness* (New York, 1954), in which he examines the symbolic statement of hundreds of myths, seeking to establish the various stages in the emergence and evolutionary growth of the conscious ego. Another disciple, Gerhard Adler, in *The Living Symbol* (New York, 1961) gives an exhaustive account of the use of Jung's theory of dream-symbols in the treatment of a woman patient suffering from claustrophobia.

[2]*The Interpretation of Dreams*, pp. 366-367. Subsequent references to this book will be by the short title *Interpretation* and page numbers given in parentheses in the text.

[3]Ernest Jones said as much in a paper explaining the Freudian dream theory: "The manifest content is to be regarded as an allegorical expression of the underlying dream thoughts, or latent content." "Freud's Theory of Dream," *Papers on Psychoanalysis* (London, 1913), p. 315.

[4]*On Dreams*, pp. 111-112.

[5]*Man and His Symbols* (New York, 1968), p. 4.

[6]*The Burning Fountain*, rev. ed. (Bloomington, 1968), p. 55.

[7]*Modern Man in Search of a Soul* (New York, 1933), pp. 24-25.

[8]*The Living Symbol: A Case Study In the Process of Individuation* (New York, 1961), p. 42.

[9]*Modern Man in Search of a Soul*, p. 22.

[10]*Man and his Symbols*, p. 4.

CHAPTER FOUR

Myth As Literary Symbol

No one can attempt the perilous enterprise of writing about myth without learning the wisdom of Ernst Cassirer's remark, that of all the phenomena of human culture, myth is one of the most refractory to logical analysis. "If there is anything that is characteristic about myth," he wrote, "it is the fact that it is 'without rhyme and reason . . .' It defies and challenges our fundamental categories of thought."[1] We have, to begin with, a severe problem with the term itself which, like the word "symbol," seems to represent something with which this century has been fascinated to the point of obsession, though it may be beyond human capability to say just what that something is. "Myth" has acquired, like "symbol," so many conflicting meanings that it has virtually ceased to have definable meaning.[2] And yet the obsession remains. In recent years the pursuit of mythic paradigms, archetypes, allusions, and fragments in literature has become a major academic industry, and the sleuths of myth so sedulous that it is a rare writing indeed which can conceal its goat foot for long. Hardly an action in story or poem can escape being seen as a *ritual* action, hardly a journey which is not a "quest," hardly a struggle or a moment of suffering which is not some rite of passage, hardly a character who is not a scapegoat, an earth mother or a vegetation god. Many of our most admired writers have been admired because they were thought to be most "mythic," or "mythopoeic," or often in the same breath, most "symbolic."

71

Nietzsche thought that all our myth-mongering is a sign that modern man is *mythless* man, eternally grubbing in the past for roots. "The stupendous historical exigency of the unsatisfied modern culture," he wrote, "the gathering around one of countless other cultures, the consuming desire for knowledge—what does this point to, if not to the loss of myth, the loss of the mythical home, the mythical source?"[3] Certainly the loss of the mythic past is a major theme of many modern poets. T. S. Eliot tried in both poetry and criticism, with something like desperate urgency, to throw a bridge across the gulf which separates modern Western man from his traditional home in Christian myth. Wallace Stevens wrote over and over again of "the swans whose bills are flat on the ground," of "the waltzes which have ended," of "empty heaven" and "the rotted names." W. B. Yeats spent his mature lifetime searching the quagmires of occultism and the enchanted forests of the Irish mythic past for ground upon which his own displaced soul might come to rest.

It would be tempting simply to turn away from "myth" entirely as a term too blurred or tangled to be useful, except that we have no other which can serve as well to represent whatever it is that so fascinates us. But perhaps if we were to adopt the opposite tactic, if we were to turn and face the ambiguity, accepting it because we cannot avoid it, perhaps then the ambiguity itself might speak to us, revealing something of what it seems to obscure. To do this, it is necessary to recognize that "myth" is not one thing but a number of things, that it does not have one meaning but encompasses a whole area of meanings, that it will not yield to aggression nor to the frontal attack of any single definition, but must be sidled up to, looked at askance and with amiable openness, before it will unveil any part of its mystery. "Tell all the truth," said Emily Dickinson, "but tell it slant. Success in circuit lies." So in this essay with chastened and proper modesty, I will walk around the area of meaning called "myth," inquiring into its relationship with two other areas of meaning called "symbol" and "poetic," willing to settle from the outset for something less than final answers to the questions I put.

Some Conflicting Theories of Myth

Without trying to survey all of the many theories of myth, it will be helpful to mention several which literary critics have made most use of—at times rather uncritical use. I will suspend my own attempt at definition until I have cited these others.

Myth comes into literary criticism with the romantic criticis such as Novalis, Schelling, and Goethe, but first becomes a major shibboleth with the writings of a group of classical anthropologists at Cambridge University, beginning in the 1880's. Among this group are Jane Harrison, A. B. Cook, F. M. Cornford, Gilbert Murray (from Oxford), and best-known of all, Sir James Frazer, whose monumental work *The Golden Bough* (1907-1915) stirred an entire generation of poets. This group of scholars developed an influential theory of myth called the "ritual" or "survival" theory, which in its broad outlines sees human culture as subject to a process of evolution in which religious, magical, or social rituals gradually die out and are replaced by fictive substitutes or myths.[4] "Myth is a fiction," wrote Frazer, "devised to explain an old custom, of which the real meaning and origin had been forgotten."[5] These scholars were able to demonstrate that many aspects of both form and content in Greek epic and drama are survivals of earlier ritual practices. The very form of the theater itself, the number of actors, the origin and function of the chorus, the divisions of the drama into its various parts, and many specifics of content, are among such survivals.

Other theories and definitions of myth come in all sizes, shapes, and flavors these days, nearly as many theories as theorizers, the flavor of a theory usually depending upon the background and training of the theorizer, upon whether he speaks as anthropologist (several kinds here), sociologist, psychologist (several kinds here too), philosopher, art historian, theologian, and the like. Especially important are the psychological or psychoanalytical theories, and here as with so much else in depth psychology, Freud was first. In *Totem and Taboo* (1912) he proposed that myths originate in neurosis and are to society what dreams are to the individual. He assumed that the contents of myth resemble the contents of the unconscious, and that man in his evolution has passed through a primordial mythopoeic age (still experienced by contemporary primitive peoples) in which he lived wholly or chiefly in the unconscious, consciousness being a relatively late acquisition in man's psychic development. The same dynamics of the psyche which produce neurosis and dreams in individuals produce their collective counterparts—ritual and myth—in society, and myths

73

serve the same protective and restorative functions for society that dreams serve in the individual.

Freud promulgated a version of the Oedipus story as a way of describing archaic experiences which resulted in the universal feeling of guilt with which all men are haunted. The story tells of a Primal Horde, ruled over by a violent and powerful father, who wished to keep all the females for himself and drove out all the adolescent sons. But the sons, infuriated by their sexual frustrations, banded together and killed the Primal Father and ate him. Then overcome by remorse, for they had also loved and admired him, they set up incest taboos as penance and formed a system of totems in which symbolic animal substitutes for the father would be fostered and propitiated by rites of worship and sacrifice.[6]

A second psychological theory of major importance is that of C. G. Jung, who accepted the Freudian theory in general outline, but placed less emphasis upon neurosis and repression as the underlying causes of myth. His fundamental innovation was an assumption that myths are produced by the unconscious not only in connection with previously repressed material, but are also produced *spontaneously* by the great formative principles and tendencies of the collective unconscious which he called the *archetypes*. These mysterious archetypes, as we have previously noted, are unknowable directly, but can be known indirectly through symbolic images which they send up, and which appear in various media such as dreams, fairy tales, folklore, literature and the other arts, and importantly in myths. "Mythic" for Jung virtually translates "archetypal," a myth being a story of traditional and collective social significance carrying important archetypal symbolic content. In this view, a dream, a painting by Leonardo, an opera by Mozart, or a novel by Tolstoi, to the degree that it is expressive of the archetypes, could be as "mythic" as the Greek stories about Prometheus or Odysseus. Archetypal or mythic material is by definition "numinous," or highly charged with psychic energy, so that when it passes over into consciousness it is felt as revelation or as a compelling, deeply emotional experience which moves one to some kind of total response. Because myths contain, like other symbolic expressions of the unconscious, both a conscious component and an unconscious component, Jung saw them serving a bridging or mediating function as one instrument of the growth and development of the human psyche.

One branch of modern anthropology, which can be well represented by Bronislaw Malinowski (1884-1942) has urged a "functionalist theory" of myth. Malinowski insisted that the study of myth should not be confined to written texts, but should include what he called "live" myth in its living context, the kind which he himself had collected during extensive field trips in the Trobriand Islands north of New Guinea. "Studied alive," he wrote, "myth . . . is not symbolic, but a direct expression of its subject-matter, a narrative resurrection of primeval reality . . . It expresses, enhances, and codifies belief; it safeguards and enforces morality; it vouches for the efficiency of ritual and contains practical rules for the guidance of man."[7] Malinowski distinguished three kinds of mythic stories: fairy tales or folktales, which are told simply for amusement; legends, which provide a tribe with its history; and religious myths, which provide accounts of the origin of things and the basis for proper moral and social conduct.

Several developments in ancient Greece are of greatest importance to a consideration of the symbolic dimension of myth: first of all, the fact that a large body of mythic stories was given high literary form by Homer and Hesiod; and second, a development apparently unique in world culture, the fact that this entire body of stories was subjected to persistent rational or allegorical interpretation of several kinds, beginning at least by the 6th century B.C. As a result, these myths were effectively emptied of religious content, and myth, instead of signifying a sacred story containing life's deepest meanings, came to mean a fiction, a mere fiction, something not to be believed.[8] The best-known of the skeptical approaches to myth goes by the name of Euhemerism, after Euhemerus (fl. 300 B.C.), who proposed that myths are a kind of decayed history, that such people as Helen, Achilles, and Agamemnon in the Atreus myth are based upon real people, that the heroic events in the *Iliad* reflect an actual military expedition. Closely related are the causal or etiological theories, which see myth as a kind of primitive metaphysics or science. The identification of Zeus with the sky and with lightning, of Aphrodite with the erotic impulses, or Aries with the warlike instincts, are seen as naive attempts to explain the otherwise mysterious workings of nature or of human nature. The early fathers of the Christian church found such allegorical methods of interpretation ready at hand when somewhat later they looked for means of discrediting any part of the pagan mythic tradition not in accord with Biblical authority. And paradoxically, because they were thus deprived of religious content, the old stories of Homer and Hesiod and the entire Greek and Roman pantheon survived the Christian Middle Ages and lived on into modern times as a major cultural force.[9] But from an early time two ideas were fastened firmly upon the Western mind: (1) that myth is a function of literature; and (2) that myth is symbolic, a writing whose surface statement is not to be taken literally, but must be penetrated or interpreted so as to uncover the true meaning hidden beneath.

Some of the more recent allegorical readings of myth have been extraordinary. In the nineteenth century Winckler and others argued that most myths, no matter what their surface statement, are directly or indirectly *moon* myths; Leo Frobenius argued that most are *sun* myths; Max Müller, using word etymologies and comparative philology, argued that most are *sky* myths. Immanuel Velikowsky, who wrote the sensational *Worlds in Collision* (1950), represents a more recent Euhemerism, which sees Biblical and other flood or catastrophe myths as the notation of actual worldwide disasters caused by the near-miss of an alien planetary body wandering too close and disturbing earth's gravitational poise. Hans Hörbiger, writing after World War I, cited dozens of moon-myths to authenticate a fantastic theory that the earth has had a number of ice-coated moons which have plunged one at a time from orbit and struck the earth with catastrophic effect. Hitler is said to have been a zealous believer in the Hörbiger Cosmic Ice Theory, which had through his agency a major and tragic impact on world events of the 20th century.

The Mythopoeic Mind

Whether there was ever a "mythopoeic age," as the depth psychologists and some others claim, several French anthropologists such as Durkheim and Lévy-Bruhl, and philosophers such as Cassirer and Wheelwright, have described a "mythopoeic mind," a mythic way of viewing reality. "Myth, then," wrote Philip Wheelwright, "is not in the first instance a fiction imposed on one's already given world, but is a way of apprehending that world. Genuine myth is a matter of perspective first, invention second."[10] Seen in this fashion, myth becomes a function of epistemology, a function of a mythopoeic mind, which is usually taken to be about the same thing as the archaic or primitive mind. Because of a cultural tradition which has emphasized analytic, conceptual, "scientific" modes of thought, modern Western man has diverged radically from the mythic way of seeing, though he still has links to it in the religious and poetic dimensions of his mind. Ernst Cassirer assumed myth to be one of the autonomous symbolic modes of perception, parallel with language, mathematics, law, and the arts, a way of seeing which posits a world of its own. The following brief summary of the mythopoeic perspective, as all such discussions must be, is heavily in his debt.[11]

To begin with, the man who sees the world in mythic perspective feels himself and his world as one; he belongs to his world and it to him. He does not separate himself out in Cartesian fashion as a subjective consciousness viewing from his private perspective a world of objects "out there." He is moved by what Lévy-Bruhl called the *participation mystique*, an urgent compulsion to merge his own being with that of the world around him, whether of society or of nature. His world is made up of "presences" which he experiences not as ideas or concepts, but as intense sensuous impressions, each of which he feels with a preemptive concentration which causes all other surrounding things to dwindle. Everything in his world is permeated by a spiritual energy or *mana*—every person, or tree, or stream, every configuration of his world, giving off its own quality and degree of this universal spiritual force. He experiences every part of his world with empathy—or to use Cassirer's word, physiognomically—that is, under the aspect of some strong personal emotional tone or atmosphere, whether benign or malignant, repellent or fascinating, alluring or terrifying. In Buber's phrase, each part of his world stands as a *Thou* to his *I*.

Because he does not conceptualize his world, or classify it into separate categories or static shapes, he experiences a reality which is fluid and in constant change. By a pervasive law of *metamorphosis*, any thing within this world can suddenly become any other thing. The laws of specific cause and effect familiar to the scientific mind are inoperable in the world of mythic consciousness, but another law operates in their stead. Any juxtaposition, any collocation of simultaneous events, can serve as a mythic "cause." The swallow comes with spring, therefore the swallow causes spring. A woman becomes pregnant shortly after walking near a certain grove of trees, therefore the pregnancy has been caused by the daimon of the grove. Anything can come from anything because anything can stand in temporal or spatial contact with anything. Mythical thinking clings only to total representations as such and contents itself with picturing the simple course of what happens.

To the man viewing the world in mythic perspective, "quantity" is a relatively insignificant property of things, but "quality" is all-important. He therefore can regard every part of a whole as the whole itself and every specimen as equivalent to an entire species. The drops of water sprinkled on the ground in a rainmaking ceremony are felt to contain the whole nature and quality of the rain itself. A picture of a man or a paring of his fingernail or a bit of his hair *is* the man himself. In this world, time is biological, cyclic, and seasonal rather than segmented and sequential. The flowering of plants, the cycles of daylight and dark, the phases of the moon, the seasons of the year are the means by which time is apprehended, concrete events which nevertheless have a recurrent dependability and therefore a timelessness. Myths themselves are characteristically set in an indeterminate time, an apocalyptic or paradisal future, or more often a timeless past, "in the beginning," or "once upon a time," or "in the time of our fathers."

Mircea Eliade claims that the greatest difference in outlook between modern and primitive man has to do with the time sense.[12] Whereas modern man thinks of himself as produced by, and as bound to an irreversible, chronological sequence of events called history, primitive man, though aware of a sequence of history, believes that by reciting the sacred myths of origin he can emerge from profane time and enter another time, an eternal moment which is at once primordial and indefinitely recoverable. What is involved is not a commemoration of mythical events, but a reiteration of them of the kind which the Roman Catholic church has always claimed for the mass. Thomas Mann, in his lecture, "Freud and the Future," described the mythic way of seeing as a tendency to view life in terms of timeless schemata or patterns, the ability to see one's own existence as a fresh incarnation of some typical or traditional paradigm, to see life as a sacred repetition. He cites as example Napoleon, seeing himself fulfilling the role of Alexander or Charlemagne, not merely resembling Charlemagne, but being him through living the same archetypal role of warrior-king; or Jesus consciously living out the prophetic specifications of the god-man who gives himself in sacrifice; or Paul with sudden and blinding compulsion committing himself to the role of God's messenger.

Finally, we should mention the "structuralist" theory of myth promulgated by the French anthropologist Claude Lévi-Strauss, which has aroused considerable interest among literary critics since World War II.[13] This theory is both epistemological and linguistic and categorically denies certain presumptions of earlier theorists like Cassirer. Cassirer had argued that myth is basically irrational and illogical, and to be distinguished from language, which is characterized by logic; he had also accepted the primacy of ritual over myth and assumed the "mythopoeic mind" of primitive man to be distinct from the logical mind of modern man. Lévi-Strauss, noting that all languages have similar features when viewed as structures, set out to show that myth has essentially these same structures. The primitive mind, he thought, is not obviously different from any other kind of human mind, but utilizes the same structure of binary opposites, proceeding always from an awareness of opposites through gradual mediation to final resolution of antinomy. A myth can be properly interpreted only when related to its own ethnography and can best be interpreted when studied in relation to a larger group of other myths from the same area.

There are other approaches to a theory of myth besides the ones we have sampled, but perhaps we have seen enough of the variety and antagonism of these theories to understand some of the reasons for the blur in mythic criticism of literature. One major source of our difficulty comes from using "myth" as a general term while basing it on restricted reference. Myths are of different kinds, are quite possibly created in different ways, and certainly serve different functions. A theory derived from myth of one sort may not, when made into a general rule, apply to myths of other kinds. Jane Harrison was contemplating an archeological fragment of a hymn to Zeus when she promulgated her influential theory describing myth as *to legomenon*, "that which is spoken," which accompanies *to dromenon*, "that which is done," in a religious ritual.[14] But there is some hazard in applying this formula to such myths as those in Plato's *Dialogues*, which were created without any reference to ritual whatever. Each of the many theories of myth seems to have its partial truth, and I suspect that we shall get the highest yield in literary criticism when we learn to apply particular theories with more discrimination, and perhaps to apply a number of different theories to the same piece of literature.

A Tentative Working Definition of Myth

We have been using "myth" as a key term for some time without the benefit of a definition on the grounds that myth is too elusive a creature to capture in a single net. But it will help to ballast our discussion if we can give a tentative working definition which embraces most of the conflicting theories. In a recent book Alan W. Watts gives such a definition as follows: "Myth is to be defined as a complex of stories—some no doubt fact, and some fantasy—which, for various reasons, human beings regard as demonstrations of the inner meaning of life."[15] This defines myth not in terms of its origin, or its content, or even its function, but chiefly in terms of the way men stand toward it. It allows for secular, or political, or social myths as well as those more strictly sacred, and it permits all of the theories which have been named above. But admirable as this statement is, still it pinches with its emphasis on "meaning" and its restriction to narrative forms. I would loosen it still further and nudge it further toward the psychological as follows: *A myth is a numinous image or story.* "Numinous" here means having the power to seize men and compel them to some kind of total response, in the same sense that Jung used the word. This does not mean necessarily to instil religious faith or commitment, for some quite different response might be produced, like the violent antipathy which "communism" arouses in many Americans. "Polarize" conveys the idea, along with the idea of "power." Certain images and stories seem to act upon human beings in the way a magnetic field acts upon bits of iron, attracting some and repelling others, depending upon the strength of the field and the charge on individual particles of iron.

What makes particular stories or images numinous is, finally, a mystery. Whether a story is objectively true or not seems to have no bearing, nor whether any facts it might contain are large or small. The wildest absurdity, the most extravagant fantasy, and the flattest or most commonplace historical fact seem to serve equally well as vehicle for the mythic. And the mystery extends to why a given story

80

compels some men and not others, or why some stories or images, like those of the great religious traditions, can compel whole nations and generations of men for centuries and then lose this power.

We need to make emphatic the distinction which Malinowski and Eliade draw between the "living" myth of primitives—those functional sacred stories which set the very tone and pattern of daily existence—and the "great mythologies" of literate, historical societies, which have been regularized and interpreted by a literary or theological tradition. It is obviously myths of the latter kind with which we are most involved here, but we need to beware simplistic categories. Myths are numinous in varying degrees, as they are "living" or functional in varying degrees, and these variations depend upon complex factors. It might be argued that Americans in the 20th century, instead of being a mythless people are a myth-ridden people. Our mythic substrate consists of many secular images and stories such as those associated with the Revolution and the epic settlement of the West; certain people like Washington, Franklin, and Lincoln; sacred documents such as the Constitution and the Declaration of Independence; certain pastoral images like those of the sturdy yeoman farmer and the frontier scout; an elaborate tradition of Judaeo-Christian stories; and of course the Greek myths, the Norse myths, and assorted Celtic, Indian, or other myths. Which of these are functional and which are "dead" is infinitely negotiable depending upon the individual. In our print culture all are "literary," though some are more literary than others, most of all the Greek and the Judaeo-Christian stories, since these have had longest passage in our literature. The Judaeo-Christian stories are still functional for millions of Americans, the Greek stories not, though it is hard to imagine that our lives have been unaffected by stories so deeply imbedded in our language and thought over so many centuries.

How one tests for numinosity in an image or story is equally problematic. The only test which strikes me as at all useful is the venerable one of *consensus gentium*, the agreement of peoples. If an image or story keeps popping up; if it appears in numerous variant forms; if in fact it fascinates and produces powerful response in many people, especially if it does these things over a long time and for large numbers of people, then it probably has numinosity and is mythic.

Mythic Story vs. Mythic Image

Myth is commonly assumed to take the form of narratives, but it will save confusion if we recognize that quite as often it takes the form of discrete images, which have the same numinous power as mythic stories but a less specified direction and potential. Hitler polarized Germany in the 1930's with a number of such images—the blond Aryan super race, the scapegoat Jew, the prophetic, infallible leader. Americans for some 300 years have floated upon a cluster of numinous images, a version of the Earthly Paradise called the American Dream; and for the past hundred years millions of people in many parts of the world have felt the power of a more sombre cluster of images, a different version of the Earthly Paradise, called the Classless Society or the Dictatorship of the Proletariat.

The difference between a mythic image and mythic narrative is something like the difference between a snapshot and a movie. Mythic images have no time-line; whereas mythic narratives participate meaningfully in space-time, sharing with the objective world such characteristics as continuity, duration, and pattern. Without in the least being able to prove it, I am inclined to think that mythic images come first in the order of things and mythic narratives later. Mythic images exist rather like grammatical subjects which have no predicate; mythic narratives give such images predication, habituating them to space-time and to the other boundaries of human consciousness and capability. The knight-errant of medieval chivalry, combining heroic warrior virtues in unstable combination with Christian virtues of chastity, humility, and charity, has been a powerful mythic image in Western culture, an image whose meanings have been searched out over many centuries in numberless narratives. Such images are extremely durable (Jung taught that they are imperishable) and capable of assuming many different forms or protective colorations in order to survive. No doubt the image of the knight-errant is itself a version of an older image of the warrior hero, a mutation habituating it to Christian surroundings. Mythic images have many of the characteristics of fixed symbols, but by no means all symbols nor all images are mythic. Keats' image of the wine cup, the "beaker full of the warm South . . . With beaded bubbles winking at the brim/ And purple-stained mouth," is marvellously vivid in sensuous ap-

82

peals, and darkly symbolic of easeful death, but it has never, like the Holy Grail, drawn the eyes and aspirations of uncounted thousands over many years.

Myth and Literature

Functional myth for any society is carried in the entire fabric of daily life, in social behavior, in clothing styles, in song and dance, in architecture and the fine arts, in the practical arts; and this is as true for an industrial, urbanized society as for a tribe of food-gatherers in New Guinea. But as we have seen, in the Western cultural tradition, whatever the functional myths might be which determined men's lives, there has been another overlay of myth which has been closely associated with literature. In ancient Greece the relationship was so close that the word *mythos* meant simply a story, fable, or fiction, and Aristotle in the *Poetics* used the word in this sense to designate the plot or narrative component of a tragic drama, as opposed to theme or idea which he designated by *logos* or *dianoia*. The old mythic stories provided the Greek poet with the main substance of situation, event, setting, and even of character, that is, with a *donnée* (to use Henry James' term) of great depth and richness, universally known and felt by his audience. The poet's contribution was understood to consist of creative interpretation and adornment of such known materials, a literary process in which myth was expected to be used as the vehicle for serious social, moral, or religious ideas.

Because mythic narratives have the same format and constituent elements as other narratives (character, setting, action, and often dialogue) they bear an obviously close relationship to poetic. One way to describe this relationship is to say, as Mark Schorer has done, that "myth is the indispensable substructure of poetry,"[16] which sees myth as prior raw material without which there could be no literature. We could have no *Iliad* without demigods like Achilles, no *Paradise Lost* without the celestial rebellion of Lucifer and his demonic host. But Richard Chase has argued the completely opposite view, that "poetry is the indispensable substructure of myth. Myth is a less inclusive category than poetry. Poetry *becomes* myth when it performs a certain function." He feels that myth is simply any literature which discovers and presents the preternatural, any literature which has *mana*. And this means any literature which has "impersonal magic force or potency, and is therefore extraordinarily beautiful, terrible, dangerous, awful, wonderful, uncanny, or marvelous."[17]

We can give this top still another spin by claiming with Francis Fergusson that without literature there would be no myth. He insists that there is no such thing as Ur-myth or myth-in-general, like the stories we read in Bulfinch or Edith Hamilton. Such myths are editorial composites, made up by someone like Bulfinch from a number of separate literary versions. In actuality, all we have are the *separate* literary versions, like the Oedipus of Sophocles, or the Oedipus of Seneca, Dryden, or Gide, which are different from one another. Claude Lévi-Strauss cuts the Gordian entanglement of myth and poetic by a simple formula: "Poetry is a kind of speech which cannot be translated except at the cost of serious distortions; whereas the mythical value of the myth remains preserved, even through the worst translation. Whatever our ignorance of the language and culture of the people where it originated, a myth is still felt as a myth by any reader throughout the world. Its substance does not lie in its style, its original music, or its syntax, but in the *story* which it tells."[18]

But still myth bears an important resemblance to poetic in its mode of expression. It has the same concreteness and relies in the same way upon sensuous appeals, particularly upon sensuous images. Though it may contain important conceptual or metaphysical elements, these determine its form less than the emotion from which it springs and which continuously irradiates it. It has less to do with abstract or general statements like "death is full of horror" than with images like the head of the Gorgon, its hair of snakes writhing and hissing, and the near landscape studded with immobile figures whom sight of the head has turned to stone.

Myth has often been used as a rhetorical or stylistic ornament in literature, though this is a usage more familiar to the tradition than to the present. The context of this practice is a rhetorico-poetic tradition of three styles, originating in classical antiquity and continuing unbroken in Europe until the cultural disturbances of the Romantic period. A favored means of obtaining the "heightening" which was desirable to the middle and high styles was by graceful circumlocution, often in the form of an allusion to mythology. In the first book of *The Faerie Queene* Spenser describes the sunset in words which echo the usage of Homer and Virgil:

84

Now gan the golden Phoebus for to steepe
His fierie face in billowes of the west
And his faint steedes watred in Ocean deepe.

Nearly two hundred years later, William Collins personifies Simplicity as an Attic nymph and addresses her in an apostrophe which is a tissue of mythic allusions:

O chaste unboastful nymph, to thee I call!

By all the honeyed store
On Hybla's thymy shore
By all her blooms and mingled murmurs dear,
By her, whose lovelorn woe
In evening musing slow,
Soothed sweetly sad *Electra's* poet's ear
(i.e. by the nightingale, the Philomela in Ovid's
Metamorphoses, who sang in the ear of Sophocles, who
wrote the play *Electra*.)

Usages of this kind reflect the classic or neoclassic taste for the typical and generic, but they also have pragmatic justification. In times when education was based upon the study of the classics, the mention of a single name like Apollo, Zeus, Diana, or Hercules was enough to evoke for most readers an entire mythological context, and such references could serve not only as stylistic ornament but also as a metaphoric shorthand. These conventions could be used by poets without irony at least through the eighteenth century, but sterile and perfunctory use of mythic allusion was one of the aridities of style which called forth the Wordsworthian revolt to common speech.

In spite of a distaste for the too overt use of mythic allusion, contemporary writers make as much use of myth as their neo-classic brethren, and for essentially the same literary purposes—as a metaphoric shorthand, as a storehouse of common symbolism, as vehicle for serious ideas, and as structural framework. The old myths are still told over and over again in new vernacular. Gide tells a version of the Oedipus story, Anouilh the Amphitryon, E. A. Robinson the stories of Merlin and Tristan, Marc Connolly the Noah story, Robert Frost and Archibald Macleish the story of Job, John Updike the story of Chiron the Centaur. The list is endless. The old stories obviously have the same utility for modern writers as for the ancient Greeks; they still furnish a convenient way to present universal themes deeply and instantly to a wide audience. Jean-Paul Sartre has been quoted as saying that he is always looking for myths, "in other words for subjects so sublimated that they are recognizable to everyone without recourse to minute psychological details."[19]

Among modern writers there is a distinct taste for the use of submerged or implicit myth, a classic example being Joyce's use of the *Odyssey* as a means of structuring his complex novel *Ulysses*. Eliot described Joyce's practice in 1923 in a much-quoted review: "In using the myth, in manipulating a continuous parallel between contemporaneity and antiquity, Mr. Joyce is pursuing a method which others must pursue after him. They will not be imitators, any more than the scientist who uses the discoveries of an Einstein for his own, independent, further investigations. It is simply a way of controlling, or ordering, of giving shape and significance to the immense panorama of futility and anarchy which is contemporary life."[20] Such an ordering of experience is, of course, one of the traditional functions of myth in all times and places, and is one of the reasons why poets have so frequently had recourse to it. Eliot might well approve of what Joyce was doing in *Ulysses*, since he had done something much like it, using the myth of the Fisher King to structure *The Wasteland*. Eliot insisted as a cardinal tenet of his poetic creed that a poet must ingest his entire literary tradition before he can hope to make a contribution to it, and that he must use elements of that tradition as a major portion of his own poetic language. That tradition, as we have seen, would inevitably consist in large measure of mythic materials.

The presence of irony is often a distinguishing feature of modern use of myth. One thing which gives Eliot's practice and Joyce's an edge of uniqueness is their "manipulating a continuous parallel between contemporaneity and antiquity." They set up severe ironic contrast between a past seen as heroic and a present seen as degenerate, and the mythic structure thus creates a running satire on contemporary existence. Updike pursues a similar counterpoint in *The Centaur*, as does Frost in *A Masque of Reason* and Macleish in *J. B.* Such irony, and the urge to covert rather than overt use of myth apparently provide a desired degree of objectivity, of "esthetic distance." Sister Bernetta Quinn makes the cogent suggestion that because poets of our time are reluctant to discuss directly such abstractions as Simplicity or Jealousy or Pity, in the fashion of William Collins or Thomas Gray, they turn to figures and events from myth as means of incarnating such ideas.[21] Myth feeds, in a word, the whole panoply of techniques dearest to the heart of the symbolist writer: the use of tensive, multiple levels of meaning, the use of suggestive indirection, ambiguity, paradox and irony; the interpenetration of past and present time. A symbolist era in literature is almost inevitably a myth-haunted era.

Myth as Literary Symbol

Whether a mythic image or story is symbolic or not would seem to depend largely upon how men stand toward it. According to Mircea Eliade, primitive peoples carefully distinguish between *myths*, which they consider stories of sacred content and therefore ultimately and literally true, and *fables*, which they consider stories of profane content and therefore as false or "mere" fiction.[22] We have seen how originally sacred stories recorded by Homer underwent in ancient Greece a process of allegorization, often by persons intent on preserving or enhancing their religious value, so that what was originally taken as true, came to be regarded as false, except in a symbolic sense. For the past several centuries the sacred stories of the Christian tradition have been undergoing a similar process. Don Cameron Allen has shown how the Noah story with its exact specifications for the size of the ark severely tested the ingenuity of Christian scholars for a long time to find space inside for all those pairs of animals, because Christian faith demanded that the Biblical account be accepted as literal fact.[23] Most persons today see no way to find serious "meaning" in the Noah story except by interpreting it in some symbolic fashion, that is, by treating it the same way we treat the stories of the Olympian gods. The functional life of a mythic story might be extended by its being made into a symbol, but whether or not it is symbolic is determined more by factors outside the story than those intrinsic to it.

Like other narratives, myths can make use of particular symbols. In the story of the Garden of Eden given in Genesis virtually all of the components have status as discrete symbols—the man, the woman, the talking snake, the tree, the apple, the garden itself, the god who walks in the garden in the cool of the day. Meanings for such symbols are created, as in a poem, not only by their tensive relationships within the "field" of the story, but also by subjective associations brought by particular readers or hearers of the story, by factors inherent in language, by cultural and religious tradition, and, if depth psychology is to be credited, by archetypal factors from the collective unconscious which are inherent in the human psyche.

What this kind of story as a whole "means" is equally problematic and depends upon a similar complex of factors. It is obviously more than a fantastic tale about a man and a woman eating an apple on the advice of a talking snake, though this kind of fantasy is characteristic of many myths. And it seems obvious to most of us that it is something other than scientific or historical fact, though it has been read that way for many centuries, and still is by Bible fundamentalists. Only the most modest suspension of disbelief is needed to recognize that this apparently simple story speaks profoundly of deep things such as the idea of human life without pain, the relationship of man and woman, the relationship of man to authority and to the natural order, the mystery of evil, the loss of some kind of primal innocence, the awakening of the mind to conscious self-awareness, among other things. So it seems clear that such a story has symbolic value as a whole as well as in its parts, and might be said to be a symbol or a symbolic vehicle which can contain other symbols.

A myth, like other true symbols, is characterized by fecundity or symbolic pregnance, not only in the many meanings which it bears, but also in its propensity to take different forms, or to combine with the most astonishing variety of other substances. "One of the striking properties of myths," writes Francis Fergusson, "is that they generate new forms (like the differing children of one parent) in the imaginations of those who try to grasp them. Until some imagination, that of a poet, or only a reader or auditor, is thus fecundated by a myth, the myth would seem to exist only potentially."[24] The Ulysses of Tennyson, full of Faustian, nineteenth-century drive "to strive, to seek, to find, and not to yield"; the Irish, Jewish, plebian Ulysses of Joyce; and the demonic existentialist Ulysses of Kazantzakis, all different from one another, are all born out of the great-hearted Odysseus of Homer, the man who was never at a loss. The story of Oedipus is likewise Protean (to use an old-fashioned mythic allusion).

In addition to at least five different dramatic versions, the story served Freud as the suggestive center for an entire psychological system.

A myth, like other true symbols, has the "translucence" of which Coleridge spoke; through it shine hints of higher or more general or universal meanings than are recorded on its surface. Northrop Frye's definition of myth as "a conventionalized or stylized narrative not fully adapted to plausibility or realism,"[25] looks in this direction, as do many other attempts to describe the events or people in myths as "typical," or "larger-than-life." Eventually, myth moves one, like other modes of symbolism, to Baudelaire's Universal Analogy, to the Great One.

The Poet as Mythmaker

The way in which myths originate is highly problematic. Anthropologists and other social scientists tend to see them as anonymous and collective in origin. Clyde Kluckhohn, for instance, describes them as "supra-individual." "They are usually composite creations," he wrote. "They normally embody the accretions of many generations, the modifications (through borrowing from other cultures or by intra-cultural changes) which the varying needs of the group . . . have imposed."[26] Literary critics and some others like to stress more individual factors and often picture an individual shaman with vivid dreams and fantasies, or a story-teller with active imagination and a gift for spell-binding. Jung saw their origin in this fashion. "Myths go back to the primitive story-teller and his dreams," he wrote, "to men moved by the stirring of their fantasies. These people were not very different from those whom later generations have called poets and philosophers."[27] It is not difficult to cite myths or mythic figures which have been created by known authors. A good example would be Deerslayer who sprang full-armed with coonskin cap and Kentucky long rifle from the head of James Fenimore Cooper. It is possible to describe him, as recent critics have done, as a wilderness version of the Christian knight, but of his numinous power, not only for Americans but for much of the rest of the world as well, there can be little question. A more recent example of such a figure would be the Superman of the comics, who appeared, replete with a myth of origin, in 1938.

89

However they originate, myths are usually a collective phenomenon, their whole function, thrust, and power coming from, and being directed toward society as a whole, and the myths which poets use as "the indispensable substructure of literature" usually come to their hand already formed, a part of the traditional culture of society. Aeschylus, in using the myth of the house of Atreus, might alter or color the story, but he would not be the inventor of it. Even Virgil, setting out in the *Aeneid* to provide great Rome with a myth of origin, would be articulating or embroidering as much as inventing the basic myth. But in the modern world we seem to be witnessing a time when poets and artists are becoming the chief *makers* of myth. That is, at least, their own repeated testimony, and that of careful observers.

Wallace Stevens can furnish a prime example of this remarkable phenomenon, which begins in a conviction that the old gods are dead. The central theme of his poetry is an assertion, tirelessly repeated, as in *The Man With The Blue Guitar*, "Poetry/ Exceeding music must take the place/ Of empty heaven and its hymns,/ Ourselves in poetry must take their place." Only the poet and his "supreme fiction" can fill the spiritual void left by the collapse of the old myths. The first part of the poet's demanding task is to "decreate" or demythologize, to tear away whatever is left of "the rotted names." Then on the blue guitar of his poetry he must bang out a tune of "things exactly as they are," "a tune that is beyond us, yet ourselves." Stevens understood the modern time to be unique in the extraordinary pressure of reality upon the mind, a pressure unusually harsh because of the tempo and violence of industrialized civilization, and because skeptical reason has dissolved the protective buffer of myth. This violence from without must be countered by a force of imagination from within, and it is the poet who is best able among men to show how to exercise the redemptive force of imagination. "As reason destroys," he wrote in "Adagia," "the poet must create." To Stevens, God and the imagination are the same. "The final belief is to believe in a fiction, which you know to be a fiction, there being nothing else."[28]

Such statements by a great modern poet are not very different from Freud's early remark that "a large portion of the mythological conception of the world is nothing but psychology projected to the outer world."[29] And Joseph Campbell, starting from the premises of depth psychology, arrives at a conclusion about the poet's function in the modern world, which is much like that of Stevens. "There is no hiding place for the gods from the telescope and the microscope," he writes. "Society itself has changed. It is no longer a carrier of religious content, but an economic-political organization. Therefore man's problem today is opposite to that of men in the comparatively stable periods when the great co-ordinating myths were made (now known as lies). Then all meaning was in the group, none in the self-expressive individual. Today no meaning is in the group and none in the world; all is in the individual."[30] In the past the structuring and controlling myths were generated and embodied within the community, but in today's world, says Campbell, "the mythogenic zone is the individual in contact with his own interior life, communicating through his art with those 'out there.' "[31]

But to say that the poets are today's myth-makers is easier than to find the myths they have made, at least in the form of coherent narratives. Mythic images we find in plenty, like Eliot's Hollow Man and Wasteland, the terrifying rough beast of Yeats' "The Second Coming," Stevens' Major Man and the queenly personifications of his imagination, William Carlos Williams' place-god, Paterson. But few fables. The word "myth-maker," and its Greek equivalent "mythopoeic," have been freely used in recent criticism, but some of the poets to whom they have been most freely applied—like Mann, Joyce, Kazantzakis, or Eliot—seem more accurately to be myth-users. Their writings are surely steeped in myth, but in a studious, self-conscious and ingenious fashion, as if by sheer act of will one could inject myth under the skin of a poem or novel with a hypodermic needle. And one remembers the lament of Carlos Williams that Eliot in taking poetry back to the academy had set the whole thing back forty years. Williams' own instinct for the need to plunge to the bottom of the filthy Passaic, to bore a hole straight down through the native rock of Paterson, New Jersey, seems to be more promising of viable myth. Whitman knew this when he invited the muse to emigrate from Greece, and to "cross out please that old matter of Troy," and when he called the United States themselves essentially the greatest poem.

Joseph Campbell has found Joyce's *Finnegan's Wake* to be "pure mythopoeic substance," but if that is true, the book, as marvelous an accomplishment as it is, would still be only halfway to *viable* myth, whose hallmarks have usually been simplicity and availability. With all its faults, Twain's *Huckleberry Finn* would seem to be closer, as would the endless versions of Marshall Dillon clearing riff-raff from

91

the saloons of Dodge City, or Dick Tracy's or Superman's perpetual conflict against the sinister forces of evil in a modern metropolis. However little we may like to contemplate it, the fact may be that today's mythic hero may wear a badge, or a ten-gallon hat, and the myth we seek may be in sub-literature, like the Horatio Alger novels, which do tell a coherent fable, or in the TV soap operas, or in the movies or in science fiction, or in the comic strips.

It may be sheer arrogance to imagine that the myth which will seize our time will be "new" at all. Jung taught that the archetypes move as they will toward conscious expression, that the symbolic images and myths which they send up cannot be coerced, not by the most poignant yearning, and that poets cannot invent myth at all, but can only act as its channel or vessel. On the other hand, archetypal contents share the timelessness of the cosmos itself, and cannot be destroyed, though they may be warped or distorted. Eliade recently suggested that the true cultural role of the nineteenth-century novel, in spite of all the scientific, realistic, and social formulas by which it was written, was to serve as the great reservoir of debased myths.[32] And the same might be said of the twentieth-century novel. The story of Prometheus in Greek myth apparently expresses something archetypal about the indomitable nature of the human will to freedom from tyrannical and arbitrary oppression, but the expression of that archetype in our time might look more like Captain Yossarian in Heller's *Catch-22* than like the titan of antiquity.

Many poets in our time seem to be genuinely mythopoeic, not because they make frequent use of the Frazer corn-god archetype, but because they participate deeply in the mythopoeic or archaic consciousness. Poets in all ages have of course participated in this mode of consciousness, but strikingly so in the present century. I think it is not too much to claim that the modernist movement in literature represents a dramatic recovery of certain mythopoeic attitudes which had lain relatively quiescent for several centuries. One can trace a definite crescendo of the mythopoeic in literature beginning with Wordsworth's awareness of haunting presences in the nature around him; or Whitman's child starting from Paumonok and "becoming" the April flowers, the grass and the fields; or Rimbaud writing "je est un autre"; Gerard Manly Hopkins torn by conflicting allegiance to Jesuit orthodoxy and to the "haeceitas" or "thisness" of sensuous experience as expressed in his theory of inscape and instress; T. S.

Eliot castigating the "dissociation of sensibility" and straining to bring the inner and outer worlds together by means of the 'objective correlative'; Wallace Stevens saying, "The search/ For reality is as momentous as/ The search for god . . . It is the philosopher's search/ For an interior made exterior/ And the poet's search for the same exterior made/ Interior";[33] Joyce recording in a passage of intense lyric beauty a sudden epiphany—his own release from commitment to traditional Christian myth and his seizure by the sense of holiness and sacred presence of beauty in the profane world; William Carlos Williams experiencing as a young man a sudden "conversion" to the mythic way of seeing—"something," he wrote, "which occurred once when I was about twenty, a sudden resignation to existence, a despair—if you wish to call it that, but a despair which made everything a unit and at the same time a part of myself. I suppose it might be called a sort of nameless religious experience. I resigned, I gave up."[34]

If the assertions of Marshall McLuhan have validity, then our sense of loss and our search for myth may be due to our having arrived at the end of print culture and our being about to enter upon a new world based upon electronic media whose outlook resembles the archaic, mythopoeic way of seeing. Violent experimentation in all the arts would suggest that considerations of form may be of central importance to our search, or that form and substance as categories have begun to coalesce. "The style of a poem and the poem itself are one," wrote Wallace Stevens. "The style of the gods and the gods themselves are one . . . in an age of disbelief, when the gods have come to an end, when we think of them as the aesthetic projections of a time that has passed, men turn to a fundamental glory of their own and from that create a style of bearing themselves in reality."[35] The sudden emergence of the absurd, the confusion of genres, the interpenetration of various art forms, as in Wagner's music dramas, the deliberate obscurantism, the resort to irony, ambiguity, and paradox, are all signs of the search for the new style, of a feeling in the poet that the new wine cannot be carried in the old bottles. "Here I am," said E. E. Cummings' Him, "patiently squeezing four dimensional ideas into a two dimensional stage."

Over and over our poets tell us that to discover living truth we must become "natives of earth," that we must reach into "the foul rag and bone shop of the heart." Thoreau discovered a hundred years ago at

Walden Pond that "we must find our occasions in ourselves" and that "God culminates in the present moment." And much longer ago than that, while the Pharisees scanned the horizon for a messiah, Jesus kept telling them, "I am the man. The kingdom of God is among you and within you." Seen in this light, Wallace Stevens' repeated declaration that God and the imaginer are the same sounds less like blasphemous egoism than like a rediscovery of the ancient oriental way of spiritual enlightenment—the awakening to an awareness that Atman, or the essential self, and Brahman, the universal spirit of the cosmos, are one and the same.

And so our circle closes; our circuit of myth has brought us around, as we said it would, to the Great One. We started our circuit with the purpose of discovering how myth functions as a mode of symbolism in literature, and now we should reassert some of the things we found: (1) that myth is not one but many, and that to ask questions about its symbolic status we need at least to distinguish "functional" from "literary" myth; (2) that myth takes the form of unpredicated images as well as of sequential narratives; (3) that myth is symbolic depending upon how men stand toward it; that literary myth is usually taken to be *essentially* symbolic, while functional myth is seldom regarded a symbolic; (4) that literary myth is thus a lesser category of both literature and symbol; (5) that poets in the past have usually been transmitters of traditional myth, but that today's poets, though they make much use of traditional myth, often see themselves as *makers* of myth.

But most of all we have seen how furtive and evasive is myth to rational inquiry. We came with our little candle to explore a great mystery, and if we have seen light flash from one or two of its curious facets, I doubt that we have been permitted to see very far into its dark center.

Footnotes to Chapter IV

[1] *An Essay on Man* (New Haven, 1944), p. 73.

[2] Three gatherings of essays on myth are useful: Henry A. Murray, ed. *Myth and Myth-Making* (Boston, 1968); Thomas A. Sebeok, ed. *Myth: A Symposium* (Bloomington, 1958); and John B. Vickery, ed. *Myth and Literature* (Lincoln, Nebraska, 1966). For discussions of the many meanings of "myth" as a term in literary criticism, see Wallace W. Douglas, "The

94

Meaning of 'Myth' in Modern Criticism," *Journal of Aesthetics and Art Criticism*, 11 (1952), 46-54. [Reprinted in Vickery, pp. 119-136]; David Bidney, "Myth, Symbolism, and Truth," *Journal of American Folklore*, 68 (1955), 379-392. [Reprinted in Sebeok, pp. 3-24, and in Vickery, pp. 3-13]; Haskell M. Block, "Cultural Anthropology and Contemporary Literary Criticism," *Journal of Aesthetics and Art Criticism*, 11 (1952), 46-54. [Reprinted in Vickery, pp. 129-136]; Richard Chase, *Quest for Myth* (Baton Rouge, La., 1946).

[3] *The Complete Works of Friedrich Nietzsche,* ed. Oscar Levy (1909-1911), 18 vols. Reissued 1964, I, 175.

[4] For an excellent account of the ritual theory, which includes a running bibliography of the major writings, both first and second generation, see S. E. Hyman, "The Ritual View of Myth and the Mythic," in Sebeok, pp. 136-153. [Reprinted in Vickery, p. 47-58].

[5] James G. Frazer, *The Golden Bough* (London, 1915), IV, 153.

[6] For a good brief survey of Freudian theory, see Patrick Mullahy, *Oedipus: Myth and Complex: A Review of Psychoanalytic Theory* (New York, 1948).

[7] "Myth in Primitive Psychology," in *Magic, Science and Religion* (New York, 1954).

[8] For a fuller account of these events, see Mircea Eliade, *Myth and Reality* (New York, 1963), esp. chapter VIII.

[9] See Jean Seznec, *The Survival of the Pagan Gods; the Mythological Tradition and its Place in Renaissance Humanism and Art*. Transl. Barbara F. Sessions (New York, 1953).

[10] *The Burning Fountain*, rev. ed. (Bloomington, Inc., 1968), p. 150.

[11] Cassirer's fullest treatment of the mythopoeic perspective is *Mythical Thought*, volume 2 of the three-volume *The Philosophy of Symbolic Forms* (New Haven, 1955). Briefer treatments are to be found in *Language and Myth* (New York, 1946); *An Essay On Man* (New Haven, 1944), esp. chapter 7; and *The Myth of the State* (New Haven, 1946), esp. chapters 1-4.

[12] *Myth and Reality*, chapter 1; see also Mircea Eliade, *The Myth of the Eternal Return* (New York, 1954), p. 35.

[13] The basic statement of this approach to myth is his "The Structural Study of Myth," in Sebeok, pp. 81-106. He elaborates the doctrine considerably in later writings such as the introduction to *The Raw and The Cooked* (New York, 1964). A readable exposition of the Lévi-Strauss theory is Harold W. Scheffler, "Structuralism in Anthropology," in Jacques Ehrmann ed. *Structuralism* (New York, 1970), pp. 56-78.

[14] See her *Themis* (London, 1912), esp. the introduction and chapter 2.

[15] *Myth and Ritual in Christianity* (Boston, 1968), p. 7.

[16] Quoted in Murray, pp. 354-358.

[17]"Notes on the Study of Myth," *Partisan Review*, 13 (1946), 338-346. [Reprinted in Vickery, pp. 67-73.]

[18]"The Structural Study of Myth," in Sebeok, pp. 85-86.

[19]Quoted in Michael Grant, *Myths of the Greeks and Romans* (New York, 1962), p. 280.

[20]"Ulysses, Order, and Myth," in S. Givens ed. *James Joyce: Two Decades of Criticism* (New York, 1948), p. 201.

[21]*The Metamorphic Tradition in Modern Poetry* (New Brunswick, N. J., 1955), p. 4.

[22]*Myth and Reality*, pp. 8-11.

[23]*The Legend of Noah: Renaissance Rationalism in Art, Science and Letters* (Urbana, Ill., 1949).

[24]" 'Myth' and the Literary Scruple," *Sewanee Review*, 64 (1956), 171-185; [Reprinted in Vickery, pp. 139-147.]

[25]*Anatomy of Criticism* (New York, 1966), p. 366.

[26]"Myths and Rituals: A General Theory," *Harvard Theological Review*, 30 (1942), 79. [Reprinted in Vickery, p. 44.]

[27]"Approaching the Unconscious," in Carl G. Jung et al. *Man and His Symbols* (New York, 1968), p. 78.

[28]*Opus Posthumous* (New York, 1957), p. 163.

[29]*Basic Writings*, transl. A. A. Brill (New York, 1938), p. 651.

[30]*The Hero with a Thousand Faces* (New York, 1949), p. 387.

[31]*The Masks of God: Creative Mythology* (New York, 1960), p. 93.

[32]Mircea Eliade, *Images and Symbols*, transl. Philip Mairet (New York, 1961), p. 11.

[33]*Collected Poems* (New York, 1964), p. 481.

[34]*Selected Letters*, ed. John C. Thirlwall (New York, 1957), p. 147.

[35]*Opus Posthumous*, p. 209.

CHAPTER FIVE

Six Hallmarks of the Symbolist Mode

It is not the use of symbols which makes a writing *symbolist*, not even the use of many symbols, for the most photographically realistic writing can use symbols. It is rather a particular stance of the writer toward reality and toward his art, an involvement in attitudes and ideas which are associated with the organic world view which first emerged near the end of the eighteenth century, and in the organic symbolism which grew out of that world view. In briefest terms, symbolist literature is writing which puts into practice what the theory of organic symbolism preaches. For good reasons, "symbolist" as a term in literary criticism is sometimes loosely equated with "modernist" and with "romantic," though as we shall see, it would probably save confusion if it were distinguished from both. Literary historians commonly contrast the symbolist mode with "allegory," which is an older and quite different kind of literary symbolism, and with "realism" and "naturalism," which are contemporaneous but quite different modes of literature stressing the empirical or positivist aspects of the modernist world view.

Much of the distinctive character of this mode derives from a unique attitude of the symbolist poet toward the symbolic medium of language, toward the function of poetry, and toward his reader. To him a poem, made of words, is meant not to instruct or entertain, to

97

transmit the cultural heritage or tell of life, but is thought to hold the power of epiphany, which is the power to embody and show forth life. To him the words of a poem are looked upon less as signs pointing to life outside the poem, than as the creative Word of Biblical tradition—the agency through which life itself comes into being. The symbolist poem is deliberately designed to force the reader out of a passive role as listener into an active role as participant in the poetic action of creation, the poem being, as Whitman said, only "clues and indirections" until the reader adds to it his own imaginative commitment and thus completes the esthetic (creative) experience.

The Enlightenment which so enormously enlarged man's power over nature was in some respects a sleep and a forgetting—so Blake called it, "single vision and Newton's sleep"—and the symbolist mode in literature represents an attempt to recover the great forgotten language which Blake called the "two-fold vision," the art of direct perception through images which had been commonplace in the pre-scientific world. "The medieval man *thought and felt* in symbols," wrote Henry Osborn Taylor in *The Medieval Mind*, "and the sequence of his thought moved as frequently from symbol to symbol as from fact to fact."[1] It is that coincidence of thought and feeling which the symbolist poet sought to revive. Single vision had meant a great expansion of the analytical reason and of the logical faculty, but also a separation of knowing subject from the known object and a separation of idea from its personal or emotional components in what Eliot called "the dissociation of sensibility." The symbolist poet, in trying to recover the "two-fold vision," seeks to bring together subject and object and to weld feeling once more to thought so that a poetic idea becomes an experience felt with the whole being, or as Yeats said, an experience "with blood, imagination and intellect running together." To achieve this extraordinary purpose, symbolist poets resorted to extraordinary literary means which it is our purpose here to describe. Most of these means can be discussed in terms of six general principles of symbolist form which we can first give briefly in a list, so that the whole pattern is visible, and then discuss more fully one at a time. For convenience we will discuss these aspects of symbolist form as if they were discrete factors which could be examined separately, but we shall find that each one more or less involves all the others, since all originate in a single mysterious center of which each is but one vector.

1. *The Principle of Impending Significance: Obscurity.*
An initial sense of density, ambiguity, or "obscurity" in meaning, along with a strong sense of further impending significance.

2. *The Principle of Indirection: Show vs. Tell.*
Rather than "tell" a message overtly, the symbolist withdraws behind a cluster of images or other nodes of literary meaning which he presents as mediate between himself and reader. These nodes, and their interaction, show forth the poem's meanings when engaged by the reader's active imagination.

3. *The Principle of Particularity: Synecdoche.*
An assumption that the largest meanings are best conveyed through sharply realized particulars of personal experience rather than through abstraction or generalization. The symbolic particle is always seen as participating in the universal meaning which it conveys. This often involves a mythic identification of words with things.

4. *The Principle of Tensive Context: Meaning as Process.* Just as all things in the universe are in the process of continual organic change, so a poem's meanings are a function of the shifting relationships between parts of the poetic "field" and interaction with a particular reader.

5. *The Principle of Variable Perspective.* In accordance with the Kantian principle of the creative imagination, since each reader brings to a poem his own unique experience of life, there will be as many versions of a poem as there are readers.

6. *The Principle of Presential Reality: Epiphany.* An assumption that natural objects can show forth through their particularity a universal presence resembling primitive *mana*, and that this presence can be caught and held in the words of a poem.

There are a number of other more specific symbolist techniques and practices which will be mentioned in later discussion, but now we can double back to our attempt at definition and reassert that a symbolist writing is one which significantly reflects the six principles given above. All works which do so will have a family resemblance to one another and will be distinct from other works which do not. The underlying theory of organic symbolism was stated, as we have seen, around the turn of the nineteenth century by great romantic critics such as Goethe, Schelling, and Coleridge, but the Romantic poets did not themselves write in the symbolist manner, nor, for the most part, did their Victorian followers. Symbolist writings did not appear in significant numbers until the 1830's, and then more in America than in Europe, for reasons which have been described by Charles Feidelson in his brilliant *Symbolism and American Literature* (1953). All of the major poets of the so-called American Renaissance—Poe, Hawthorne, Emerson, Thoreau, Melville, Whitman—were symbolists in various ways and degrees, and Poe was the first to articulate a complete symbolist esthetic. In France, Nerval was an almost exact contemporary of Poe, and Baudelaire the greatest French poet of the century, wrote in the symbolist manner in the eighteen-fifties, but the main symbolist flowering in French literature came a generation later in the eighties and nineties. In England Yeats was the first important symbolist poet, beginning in the 1890's, and after him in the present century from both sides of the Atlantic, Pound, Eliot, Thomas, Stevens, Williams, Hart, Crane, and many others as well as many novelists including Conrad, Joyce, Virginia Woolf, and Faulkner. Obviously, not all of these poets were symbolist in the same ways or in the same degree, and it must be remembered that some writers who are usually described as realists also use the symbolist manner in some ways, as in Henry James' extensive and subtle uses of controlled viewpoint and symbolic setting.

The Literary Symbol

It will be noted that we have not included the literary symbol itself among the main criteria of the symbolist mode, and that is because literary symbols are an important feature of literature in all modes and not only the symbolist. Still, there are such things as particular literary symbols, and because these are of great importance to the symbolist mode, even if not one of its main differentia, we should describe their most common forms.

100

Northrop Frye, in *Anatomy of Criticism (1957)*, has described the literary symbol as "any unit of literary structure which can be isolated for critical attention" (p. 71), and he generously includes every literary part from the printed characters on a page to individual words and phrases, to plot, character, and setting, to whole poems, stories, and dramas. He erects an impressive critical structure upon this premise, but it might also be said that it begs the question to throw every literary phenomenon whatever into a single capacious grab-bag called "symbol," because in any poem some literary elements are more "symbolic" than others, and it is critically useful to discriminate which these are. When does an element of literary structure become a symbol? I would say when it acquires a definite aura of *plus ultra* (more beyond) in terms of meaning, though this is nearly as capacious and negotiable as Professor Frye's conception. Roughly speaking, anything in real life which can be a symbol, if it can be represented by words, can be a symbol in a poem. Most commonly this would be (1) *a discrete object*, such as Wallace Stevens' blue guitar, Robert Frost's stone wall, Melville's white whale; (2) *other empirical specific*, such as the sound of Big Ben in *Mrs. Dalloway*, the smell of sea wind and evergreens in Eliot's poetry, the taste of madeleine dipped in tea in Proust's *Remembrance of Things Past*; (3) *a person*, such as Joyce's Molly Bloom, Faulkner's Sam Fathers, Wordsworth's leech-gatherer, Conrad's Kurtz; (4) *a place*, such as the house or castle in a gothic novel, Mme. de Vionnet's apartment in James' *The Ambassadors*, the sea in *Moby Dick*, the jungle in Conrad's *Heart of Darkness*; (5) *an action or event*, such as the visit to the Marabar caves in Forster's *A Passage to India*, Ethan Brand leaping into the lime kiln in Hawthorne's story, Leopold Bloom visiting the brothel in *Ulysses*; (6) *an entire plot* or some sequence of events, especially if this has the coherence of a journey or quest, though such connected sequences of action having symbolic value are more common to allegory than to symbolist writings, where plot and narrative patterns tend to be minimized. To call an entire poem, play, or story a symbol seems to me to do violence to the term. "Symbolic form" is probably more appropriate. In any case, Cassirer's principle should be invoked here, which says that a poem or novel is a symbolic form because it is an "organ of reality, an original force which produces and posits a world of its own." Obviously a symbolic form of this kind might well contain other symbols of the sort mentioned

101

above, and presumably the Cassirer principle would apply in the same way to a collection of separate stories under one cover like Joyce's *Dubliners*, or Faulkner's *Go Down, Moses*, or Anderson's *Winesburg, Ohio*, or even to a cycle of novels like Faulkner's Yoknapatawpha novels or Lawrence Durrell's *Alexandria Quartet*.

By far the most common element of verbal structure having symbolic value is the verbal image, so common in fact that there is some tendency among critics to equate image and symbol. Not all images are symbolic, though almost any image can become so through juxtaposition and repetition, principles which will be discussed at a later time. Repetition can bestow symbolic status on almost any literary part, on a gesture for example, such as the continuous references in *Portrait of the Artist* to Cranly's eating dried figs and picking his gleaming teeth. Repetition of an image, gesture, place description, or action can give it the effect of Wagnerian *leitmotiv*. Just as the Magic Fire theme, or the sound of Siegfried's hunting horn, sounded even in suggestive fragment in the midst of other musical statement, has power to evoke an elaborate complex of images and feelings in a listener, so Eliot's "lady" image, or the images of cactus and dry rock, Leopold Bloom's fragrant piece of soap, or Thomas Wolfe's "a stone, a leaf, a door" have similar evocative power within their larger poetic structures.

Modern symbolists have tended to shun as too static or too stipulated those symbolic forms dear to the Renaissance, such as the literary emblem in which a poem was written in closest correspondence with an allegorical picture, or the poem which took the form of its subject-matter, a cross, an altar, a coffin. But many modern symbolists have nonetheless invoked other more general correspondences between content and form, such as the typographical effects in the poems of Cummings and William Carlos Williams, or Eliot's use of poetic fragments to construct the *Wasteland*. Joyce displays a strong and pervasive acrostic impulse very much like that of medieval allegory, as when he works into the Aeolus section of *Ulysses* Quintilian's nine-hundred figures of speech, and employs throughout the most elaborate correspondences based upon parts of the body and elements of Homer's *Odyssey*.

But we should turn now without further preliminary to a fuller discussion of the major principles of symbolist form.

The Principle of Impending Significance: Obscurity

Poetry must resist the intelligence almost successfully.
Wallace Stevens, *OP*, p. 171.

My brain reels, but that is nothing compared with the reeling of
my readers' brains.

James Joyce, *Letters*, p. 168

Geeze, Doc, I guess it's all right but what the hell does it mean?
W. C. Williams, *Paterson*, p. 138.

The first part of one's experience with a symbolist writing is likely
to be bafflement or frustration because of a surface which seems
obscure or ambiguous, but which at the same time strongly pulls one
on with the promise of poignant significance to come. One is haunted
by the sense that he is in the presence of deep meaning which he *feels*
but cannot quite articulate. Poe records the experience in "Ligeia,"
where the narrator, peering deep into Ligeia's eyes, feels always on
the verge of penetrating the mystery they contain, like a man on the
verge of remembering something he has forgotten and cannot quite
bring to mind. "What was it?" he asked himself. "I was possessed
with a passion to know . . . How frequently, in my intense scrutiny of
Ligeia's eyes, have I felt approaching the full knowledge of their
expression—felt it approaching—yet not quite be mine—and so at
length entirely depart!" In an intense effort to break through to an
answer, his mind runs through a sequence of analogies. Ligeia's eyes
remind him of a rapidly growing vine, a moth, a butterfly, a stream of
running water, the ocean, the falling of a meteor, the glances of
unusually aged people, the telescopic sight of a star in the constella-
tion of Lyra, the sound of stringed instruments, certain passages from
books. But none of these analogies provide a way of penetrating the
mystery behind Ligeia's eyes, which remain to the last inscrutable.

Symbolist writings have this same inscrutability, and we can cite a
well-known brief passage from the first chapter of Thoreau's *Walden*
to illustrate both the atmosphere of deep meaning and the recalci-
trance:

I long ago lost a hound, a bay horse, and a turtledove, and am still on their trail. Many are the travellers I have spoken concerning them, describing their tracks and what calls they answered to. I have met one or two who had heard the hound, and the tramp of the horse, and even seen the dove disappear behind a cloud, and they seemed as anxious to recover them as if they had lost them themselves.

Readers have broken their minds on this passage for years, trying with the most persistent ingenuity to attach specifics of meaning to the apparently simple statement, but nothing in context or bibliography, in the philosophy of the period or of the man, in the words or any combination of the words, has ever yielded specific meanings that have gained anything like general assent.

The famous Jabberwocky poem from Lewis Carroll's *Through the Looking Glass* can provide another illustration of the inscrutability and ''impending significance'' of symbolist writing:

'Twas brillig, and the slithy toves
   Did gyre and gimble in the wabe;
All mimsy were the borogoves,
   And the mome raths outgrabe.

"Beware the Jabberwock, my son!
   The jaws that bite, the claws that catch!
Beware the Jubjub bird, and shun
   The frumious Bandersnatch!''

He took his vorpal sword in hand:
   Long time the manxome foe he sought—
So rested he by the Tumtum tree,
   And stood awhile in thought.

And as in uffish thought he stood,
   The Jabberwock, with eyes of flame,
Came whiffling through the tulgey wood,
   And burbled as it came!

One, two! one, two! And through and through
  The vorpal blade went snicker-snack!
He left it dead, and with its head
  He went galumphing back.

"And hast thou slain the Jabberwock?
  Come to my arms, my beamish boy!
O frabjous day! Callooh! Callay!"
  He chortled in his joy.

'Twas brillig, and the slithy toves
  Did gyre and gimble in the wabe;
All mimsy were the borogoves,
  And the mome raths outgrabe.

This poem is a virtual parody or caricature of the symbolist poem. It has a madcap mixture of whimsy and terror, a tantalizing hint of meaning which constantly eludes, and the strange word-coinages—"slithy toves," "mome raths,"—which foreshadow Joyce's later adventures with words. Alice herself makes the appropriate comment: " 'It seems very pretty,' she said when she had finished it, 'but it's *rather* hard to understand!' (You see she didn't like to confess, even to herself, that she couldn't make it out at all.) 'Somehow it seems to fill my head with ideas—only I don't exactly know what they are!' "

That precisely describes the initial impact of a symbolist writing.

When Poe first formulated a complete symbolist esthetic in the 1830's and 40's, he included as one of its main parts "indefiniteness" as being more suggestive and thus more poetic than the definitive or realistic literary statement. His own chief means of obtaining this quality in his poems and stories was by a deliberate blurring of the outlines of the world of his poem, using such phrases as "out of space, out of time," "misty mid-region of Weir," "Night's Plutonian shore," and adjectives like "dark," "vast," "boundless," "shoreless," and the like. Such usages, like Baudelaire's synesthesia or Rimbaud's "tout dérèglement des sens," or the deliberately induced flame-lit darkness of the Wagnerian operas, were meant to neutralize or baffle the rational consciousness so as to carry the reader into the realm of waking reverie, on the theory that this state of subliminal consciousness gives most immediate access to the Supernal Beauty which was the chief end sought in the poems.

In an early chapter in *Moby Dick*, Melville seems consciously to be examining this phenomenon of indefiniteness which sets up in the beholder an obsessive urge to discover a crucial meaning which constantly eludes. As Ishmael enters the Spouter Inn in New Bedford, he sees on one wall a very large oil painting "so thoroughly besmoked, and every way defaced" that even by repeated study he could not make out what it represented—"a boggy, soggy, squitchy picture, truly." Like the narrator in Poe's "Ligeia," he begins to scan for suitable analogies: it's the Black Sea in a midnight gale, the unnatural combat of the four primal elements, a blasted heath, a Hyperborean winter scene. But none of these darts of meaning will suffice, and so Ishmael settles for the theory that the picture represents "a Cape Horner in a great hurricane; the half-foundered ship weltering there with its three dismantled masts alone visible; and an exasperated whale, purposing to spring clean over the craft, is in the enormous act of impaling himself upon the three mastheads." It is not the least of Melville's ironic insights that the interpretation which Ishmael finally settles on is no less impenetrable than the painting itself. But the kind of deliberately induced vagueness represented by Ishmael's boggy, soggy picture is less common among later symbolists than an inscrutability imparted by brightly-lit particulars rendered in the hard, clear, precise manner of the imagist poets, a practice about which we shall have more to say in a later section.

What we have here called "impending significance" Jung and Cassirer both call "symbolic pregnance" as a way of suggesting the symbol's meaningful plenitude. In his excellent book *The Literary Symbol* (1955), William York Tindall calls this same characteristic "immanent or embodied analogy," and finds it to be one of the chief differentia of the symbolist mode. "A symbol," he writes, "seems a metaphor one half of which remains unstated and indefinite." (p. 12) It is that unstated half of the metaphor which creates the pull on the reader to complete the meaning. In the final scene of *Death in Venice*, for example, Mann describes in a single sentence an unattended camera standing on its tripod on the beach its glassy eye pointed seaward, its black cloth fluttering in the freshening wind. Only this single reference to any camera. No comment and no hint of its relevance. As he contemplates this image, the reader is left, as it were, standing on one foot, urgently looking for the place to put the other foot down so he can stand at ease.

Symbolist poets have always made a great deal of the various sub-rational or subliminal appeals to a reader and use such words as "atmosphere" and "tone," to describe this poetic dimension. Conrad, for example, stressed "tonality" in his author's note to *Heart of Darkness*: "That sombre theme," he wrote, "had to be given a sinister resonance, a tonality of its own, a continued vibration that, I hoped, would hang on the air and dwell in the ear after the last note had been struck." And Whitman, in *Specimen Days*, spoke of placing the reader in the "atmosphere" of a poem: "At its best," he wrote, "poetic lore is like what may be heard of conversation in the dusk, from speakers far or hid, of which we get only a few broken murmurs. What is not gathered is far more—perhaps the main thing." Hawthorne was aware of this kind of "affective" meaning. Near the end of *The Scarlet Letter* there is a scene where Hester stands outside a church in which Dimmesdale delivers his last sermon. She cannot hear his words, but only his voice as it rises and falls, conveying to her an elaborate but wordless kind of meaning. "The poem reveals itself," says Stevens in "Adagia," "only to the ignorant man." And Faulkner asserts this idea in many places: "That is the substance of remembering," says Miss Rosa in *Absalom, Absalom*, "—sense, sight, smell: the muscles with which we see and hear and feel—not mind, not thought: there is no such thing as memory: the brain recalls just what the muscles grope for: no more, no less . . ."[2]

The various devices of musicality in literature—alliteration, assonance, rime, rhythmic effects of all kinds, and simple repetitions of verbal elements in the manner of Wagnerian *leitmotiv*—are of especial use to such subliminal appeals. There is considerable evidence that Poe, for example, thought of his poems as acting literally like charms or incantations, through such means. And John Senior has argued convincingly that some symbolist poems, like those of Mallarmé, seem to be intended to act like *yantras*, those symbolic designs used by oriental occultists to assist the process of meditation by unhinging the mind from its customary anchors to physical reality and freeing it to penetrate to visionary realms.[3] "The purpose of rhythm in poetry," wrote Yeats, "is to prolong the moment of contemplation, the moment when we are both asleep and awake, which is the one moment of creation, by hushing us with an alluring monotony, while it holds us waking by its variety, to keep us in that state of perhaps real trance, in which the mind liberated from the pressure of the will, is unfolded in symbols.''[4]

Always the symbolist comes back to the *words*, to the magic power of language to stir something deep within a reader which Poe called ''an elevating excitement of the soul,'' and always this something struggles toward a conscious articulation which it never quite achieves. Fitzgerald describes the experience with great poignance and beauty at the end of the sixth chapter of *The Great Gatsby*: ''Through all he said . . . I was reminded of something,'' says Nick Carraway, ''—an elusive rhythm, a fragment of lost words that I had heard somewhere a long time ago. For a moment a phrase tried to take shape in my mouth and my lips parted like a dumb man's, as though there was more struggling upon them than a wisp of startled air. But they made no sound, and what I had almost remembered was uncommunicable forever.''

II

The Principle of Indirection: Show vs. Tell

Don't state—render.
Henry James

The ''impending significance'' of the symbolist writing, that obscurity and the pull toward meaning which we have just described, is related to a large scale shift in the Western mind which William Barrett has described in his book on the existentialist tradition in philosophy, *Irrational Man* (1958). ''Since the Greeks,'' he writes, ''Western man has believed that Being, all Being, is intelligible, that there is a reason for everything (at least the central tradition that runs from Aristotle through St. Thomas Aquinas into the beginning of the modern period has held this) and that the cosmos is, finally, intelligible . . . That the Western artist now finds his own inherited classical forms unconvincing and indeed almost intolerable is because of a profound change in his total attitude toward the world . . . The final intelligibility of the world is no longer accepted. Our existence, as we know it, is no longer transparent and understandable by reason . . .''

108

(p. 49) The poets themselves have said as much: "A poem need not have a meaning," wrote Wallace Stevens in *Opus Posthumous*, "and like most things in nature often does not have." (p. 177) Symbolist poems reflect this assumption that life itself is mysterious and problematic, its meanings immanent or impending, never fully knowable and never settled. They also reflect a changed attitude of the poet toward his poem and toward his reader, and therefore changed techniques of expression. "My heart aches, and a drowsy numbness pains my sense," writes Keats in the great nightingale ode, expressing his inner feeling in the overt Romantic manner. "The violin shudders like a heart that suffers . . . The sun is drowning in its own curdled blood," writes Baudelaire in "Evening Harmony," expressing the same kind of inner feeling as Keats, but withdrawing behind the images of his poem and using the disciplined indirection of the symbolist.

In *Heart of Darkness*, Conrad presents a series of images in which mechanical Western civilization is juxtaposed with the primordial world of the Congo jungle: a French warship stands offshore and shells the jungle where no visible settlement appears to exist; a great pit is blasted in a hillside, though there is no mining, no excavation, no building, and no road connected with this activity; an incredibly neat bookkeeper with high starched collar and cuffs keeps his books in "applepie order," wholly indifferent to tormented and suffering blacks groaning in the shade outside the hut; a small patched and rickety steamboat inches up the endless reaches of the Congo river, penetrating to the very heart of the mysterious jungle to a hut where Kurtz lives surrounded by a fence made of the heads of natives whom he has murdered placed on pikes. Such images, without overt commentary by the author, create a strong awareness in the reader that the heart of white civilization may not be the humanitarian idealism which first sent Kurtz into the jungle to bear the light of civilization to benighted savages, but may instead be greed and the callous brutality of white colonialism, a cruel barbarism epitomized by Kurtz's exclamation, "Exterminate all the brutes!" Such images also lead the reader to suspect, again with no overt statement by author or story, that the voyage up the great river is also a voyage into the dark recesses of the human heart—a place which Kurtz, who has penetrated its mysteries most deeply, describes as "the horror! the horror!"

Conrad's technique here is like Baudelaire's in its use of indirection. He has retired behind an enigmatic narrator named Marlow who tells the story as personal experience, with sincerity and yet with an irony which makes conclusions difficult or ambiguous. Conrad gives no diatribe about the corruption and brutality of white colonialism and no moralizing about the shallowness of human virtue and the depth of human depravity, only the images, events, and characters of the story, and the low voice of Marlow, which the reader must construe for himself.

Conrad's images work by a metaphoric principle which Philip Wheelwright has called *diaphor*, a kind of metaphor based not upon analogy but upon juxtaposition. Two things are simply placed together without comment so that each becomes involved in the other's field, thus producing a tensive area of meaning somewhere between the two which partakes of both but has its own distinct character. We can also detect here a second structural principle which might be called *the principle of cumulation or resonance*, and this simply means repeating juxtapositions of a similar kind until a definite tone or resonance is established. Joyce makes exquisite use of this principle in his story "The Dead," where he suggests the presence of death in life by a running counterpoint in which images of the coldness and whiteness of snow are juxtaposed with images of food and drink and of the hot, crowded, noisy house where the dinner party is in progress.

This kind of implied metaphor is often discoverable at more generalized levels which are usually subsumed under the terms "myth" or "archetype" in modern criticism. In "Bartleby the Scrivener," for example, Melville does not say that Bartleby is Christ or even that he is like Christ; he simply assigns to him phrase after phrase and action after action which accumulate an unmistakable resonance of particular meaning: "man of sorrow," "forlornest of mankind," "He answered nothing," "his wonderful mildness," "He was always there," "Having taken three days to meditate . . . he still preferred to abide with me." A similar cumulation conjures into hovering presence over the story the passage from Matthew 25 where Christ as judge separates the goats from the sheep. Nothing explicit in the story certifies the implication of judgment, and some elements of the story stand opposed to it; but it is hard to escape the strong implication that Bartleby is Christ or one of Christ's poor, and that the lawyer-narrator and the other persons in the Wall Street law office, that is, Wall Street itself and the civilization it represents, are under judgment in accordance with the way they react to the silent scrivener.

Symbolist indirection can best be illustrated, perhaps, by a comparison of two works, one by a poet of the traditional sort, the other by a symbolist. Until fairly recently, most writings in the Western literary tradition have been "public" in the sense that the poet's themes and ideas tended to be drawn from universally held ideas of the society, and his literary means provided by an elaborate poetic and stylistic tradition which had been codified by the rhetoricians of the ancient world and hallowed by centuries of usage. His function was traditionally understood to be some variation of the *aut prodesse aut delectare* of Horace—the poet should either instruct or please or do both at the same time. Poems written according to these assumptions continued to be written long after the theory of organic symbolism was stated by the Romantic critics; actually, they continued to dominate the literary scene until well into the present century.

To illustrate this traditional poetic mode, we can cite a poem by Longfellow entitled "Seaweed." It is important to recall that in the middle of the last century poetry was still a popular art, and that poems of this kind were a delight to unnumbered thousands of readers on both sides of the Atlantic, making Longfellow a kind of revered national hero. They were memorized, read aloud at the fireside, declaimed from school platforms, quoted on public occasions, and became in a true sense "hoarded household words." His poem is structured according to a pattern which governed many lyric poems of the last century: the poet begins with a description of some natural scene, then modulates into a statement of the "lesson" which that scene typifies.

Seaweed

When descends on the Atlantic
    The gigantic
Storm-wind of the equinox,
Landward in his wrath he scourges
    The toiling surges,
Laden with seaweed from the rocks.

111

From Bermuda's reefs; from edges
        Of sunken ledges,
In some far-off, bright Azore;
From Bahama, and the dashing,
        Silver-flashing
Surges of San Salvador;

From the tumbling surf, that buries
        The Orkneyan skerries,
Answering the hoarse Hebrides;
And from wrecks of ships, and drifting
        Spars uplifting
On the desolate, rainy seas; —

Ever drifting, drifting, drifting
        On the shifting
Currents of the restless main;
Till in sheltered coves, and reaches
        Of sandy beaches,
All have found repose again.

In these skillfully crafted stanzas, Longfellow has established his
natural scene and the controlling image of an ocean in storm. Now in a
perfectly symmetrical counterpoint, like the unfolding second wing of
a *chiasmus*, he pivots on the word "so" and with unabashed didacticism, asserts the poem's "meaning":

So when storms of wild emotion
        Strike the ocean
Of the poet's soul, erelong
From each cave and rocky fastness,
        In its vastness,
Floats some fragment of a song.

From the far-off isles enchanted,
        Heaven has planted
With the golden fruit of Truth;

112

From the flashing surf, whose vision
    Gleams Elysian
In the tropic clime of Youth;

From the strong Will, and the Endeavor
    That forever
Wrestle with the tides of Fate;
From the wreck of Hopes far-scattered,
    Tempest-shattered,
Floating waste and desolate; —

Ever drifting, drifting, drifting
    On the shifting
Currents of the restless heart;
Till at length in books recorded,
    They, like hoarded
Household words, no more depart.

                      (1845)

This poem exhibits a number of the characteristics of nineteenth-century "public" verse. It is regular, musical, discursive, with high intelligibility and low reader-demand. The central idea is familiar and readily available: that poems are made from fragments of song stirred up by storms of passion in the poet's heart. The homiletic tone is undisguised, as is the idealism which accepts without irony the familiar virtues of Hope, Courage, and Persistence as the means of overcoming life's adversities. The basic analogy upon which the poem is structured, a comparison of the poet's heart to the stormy Atlantic, is presented in a pattern which evades just enough to give the reader a satisfying sense of participation as he recognizes and unravels the poem's many symmetries.

By way of contrast, in order to illustrate that quite different principle of obliquity or indirection which is a governing principle of symbolist writing, we can cite a brief poem by Stéphane Mallarmé entitled "Salut." We should recall Mallarmé's well-known remark, cited in an earlier chapter, that to name an object directly in poetry is to kill poetic pleasure, and that true poetry lies not in statement but in allusion and indirectness, in the contemplation of images which arise from the state of reverie which a poem is meant to induce. "Salut" was composed by Mallarmé to be read at a banquet given in 1893 by the literary review *La Plume*. The poet is now an old man, revered as sage and leader of the new poetry by a circle of younger poets, who are gathered around as he lifts a glass of bubbling champagne and recites this little sonnet:

Salut

Rien, cette écume, vierge vers
A ne designer que la coupe:
Telle loin se noie une troupe
De sirènes mainte a l'envers.

Nous naviguons, ô mes divers
Amis, moi déja sur la poupe
Vous avant fastueux que coupe
Le flot de foudres et d'hivers.

Une ivresse belle m'engage
Sans craindre même son tangage
De porter debout ce salut

Solitude, récif, étoile
A n'importe ce qui valut
Le blanc souci de notre toile.

[A Toast

Nothing, this foam, virgin verse
Which merely outlines the cup;
Just as, far away, a troupe
Of sirens dives into the depths.

We sail, o my diverse
Friends, I already on the poop
You the dashing prow which cuts
The flood of thunders and winters;

A pleasant intoxication seizes me
Without even fear of the pitching
To offer standing this toast

Solitude, rocky shores, star
To whatever is worth
The white concern of our sail.]

This poem, like Longfellow's, is a discussion of the poetic process, but its method is implicit rather than explicit; it is non-discursive, with low intelligibility and very high reader-demand. While Longfellow's poem is *extensive* and sets forth its theme by generous expansion of rhetorical accretion in which one specific is added to another so as to develop a finished image and its corresponding idea, Mallarmé's poem is *intensive*, reduced almost to incomprehensibility by a severe ellipsis in which the poet systematically abstracts everything but suggestive essence. What he leaves in the poem is not a theme or message or topic but a sequence of barely suggested images which the reader must exert himself to the utmost to make sense of. Like Poe, he shuns the didactic as heretical.

Form and content to the symbolist are functions of one another, and this poem *is* what the second line says—the merest tracing of a suggestive outline. A reading of the first stanza might go something like this: "My poem, which now is presented for the first time, is a mere nothing. It is like the foaming bubbles of wine which outline the shape of this thin and fragile glass. As I look into its sensuously rounded shape, suddenly in imagination I construe a vivid image of the rounded flanks and breasts and bottoms of sea nymphs as they dive into the foaming sea." By inference, these lines *imply* a thematic meaning which might be this: The words of my poem present to me fleeting images which by analogy and by using poetic imagination I can convert into other images of vivid sensuous appeal. The flash of poetic insight is as evanescent as foam.

In the second stanza, continuing the image of the seascape evoked by imagination in the first, the poet addresses the gathering of younger aspiring poets as if all were sailing together on a ship which is their common commitment to the poet's craft—he, the elder, the captain, standing aft on the quarterdeck, they, the younger, making up the prow of the ship as it crashes through thunderous and wintry seas—the difficult times for poets, the hostile public, the rigor and pain and sacrifice of the poet to his high art.

Then in the sestet of the poem, intersecting the image of the pitching deck on a stormy sea and the idea of a pleasant glow of intoxication brought on by the wine he is drinking, so that the floor he stands on moves in vertigo under his feet, standing tall, he thrusts up his glass and offers this toast: "To solitude, rocky shores, and starlight, to whatever is worth the white concern of our sail"—which might mean something like: to the pains and dangers and high aspiration of the poet's life, and to whatever else our elite brotherhood of poets chooses to say is worthwhile. That word "white" displaced from its expected place beside "sail," and attached to the word "concern" has a multifarious gamut of suggestive meaning like that in Melville's chapter on the whiteness of the whale, ranging from purity, innocence, and virginity, to death, coldness, horror, charnel-house, and nothingness. "Sail" is a synecdoche for ship, which is in turn an image for the poet's life.

This reading of Mallarmé's poem represents only one possible interpretation; others are clearly possible. Longfellow, in the manner of the traditional poet, meant his poem to be understandable to the widest possible audience; Mallarmé, writing on essentially the same topic, and making use of imagery drawn from the same area, writes a "private" poem, intended not for a wide public, but for those few readers who share his own commitment to poetic art, and who are willing and able to undertake the extremely difficult and demanding task of creating the poem's meaning from the sparse hints given by the poet. Such a poet is not speaking for society or to it, but takes a stance over and against society and addresses himself to a coterie. His poem is not a "telling" of any kind but a "showing," a setting forth of a series of images. It does not transmit any cultural or moral heritage; it does not tell about any experience; it is meant to be an experience.

This poem is an extreme example of its kind, as is Longfellow's, and it should be understood that there are many variations and degrees of the way in which the principle of indirection is invoked. Whitman, for example, though he had gone all the way over to a symbolist posture by the time of the first edition of *Leaves of Grass* in 1855, made different use of the principle of indirection from Mallarmé. He, too, thought of his poem as mediate, designed to "indicate the pathway between reality and the soul" of the reader. As an old man looking back on his career, he said, "I round and finish little, if anything; and could not, consistently with my scheme. The reader will have his or her part to do, just as I have had mine." This is exactly the same principle which Mallarmé invokes in his verse, but nothing could be further from Mallarmé's inwardness, his painful rewriting and polishing and reduction to concentrated poetic essences than Whitman's expansiveness, his openness and frankness, his attempt to cover the whole earth and every man on it with leaves of grass.

III

The Principle of Particularity: Synecdoche

Language in a healthy state presents the object, is so close to the object that the two are identified.

T. S. Eliot, *Sacred Wood*, 149

You must remember that I don't start with an abstract notion. I start with definite images and as their rendering is true some little effect is produced.

Joseph Conrad, *Letters*, 8 Feb 99

—of this, make it of *this*, this this, this, this, this

William Carlos Williams, *Paterson*, 168

As defined by the classical rhetoricians, synecdoche meant one of the tropes, a substitution of a part for the whole, as in *spears* for *army, bread* for *food*. Such a rhetorical conception, though still applicable to the symbolist use of synecdoche, is too limited. Symbolist synecdoche is involved with other deep-seated ideas. Goethe and Schelling, it will be recalled, based their theory of the organic symbol upon the occult assumption that the Universal can be manifested only in the particulars of nature, and that therefore all natural objects have the potential symbolic power of revealing something of the Universal. The poet was urged to shun the abstract universals of the allegorical tradition, such as Justice, Prudence, Perseverance, Faith, and the like, and to start at the other end with a concrete particular like a bird, a leaf, a violet beside a mossy stone. Any such particular, with the addition of the poetic imagination, could become a *concrete universal*, an object which, as W. K. Wimsatt has said, "in a mysterious and special way is both highly general and highly particular."[5]

We should stress the importance of the poetic imagination in this process, a factor strenuously insisted upon by all symbolists from Blake to Wallace Stevens. By means of it, Blake could see the universe in a grain of sand and eternity in an hour. By means of it, Stevens believed, the poet could create his supreme fictions from the particulars of the harsh modern world. Baudelaire described this kind of imagination in an often-quoted passage from the *Journaux Intimes* as a heightened state of consciousness in the poet in which ordinary things are transfigured and their symbolic content is revealed: "In certain almost supernatural states of mind," he wrote, "the depth of life reveals itself wholly in the spectacle, as ordinary as it might be which one has under his eyes. It becomes the symbol."[6]

Fascination with the particular, sometimes with the pantheist underpinning and sometimes without it, had an astonishing currency during the last century. It was one thing which, for different reasons, romantic, realist, and symbolist all had in common. Robert Langbaum has seen in it a principle which unites nineteenth and twentieth century poetry.[7] It motivated Wordsworth's revolutionary turning to rural life and to colloquial speech, and Browning's and Hopkins' experiments with the rhythms of folk speech. It was present in the favorite idea of the American transcendentalists that microcosmic bits of matter somehow contain the secrets of the macrocosm. "A leaf, a drop, a crystal, a moment of time," wrote Emerson in *Nature*, "is related to the whole and partakes of the perfection of the whole. Each particle is a microcosm, and faithfully renders the likeness of the world." Emerson thought of the poet as the man who could see more clearly than others the cosmic or universal meanings in the particulars of the natural world. "Day creeps after day," he wrote in the *Journal* for 21 June 1838, "each full of facts, dull, strange, despised things . . . And presently the aroused intellect finds gold and gems in one of these scorned facts, then finds that the day of facts is a rock of diamonds, that a fact is an Epiphany of God . . ."

Emerson's "aroused intellect," which finds gold and gems in the mundane stuff of ordinary life, is of course the same as Baudelaire's

118

heightened consciousness, and his word "Epiphany" would become Joyce's own nearly a century later to describe his experience of the revealed glory of beauty in the profane world. Some such idea as Emerson's seems to have ignited the poet in Whitman, and he became the synecdochist *par excellence*, chanting in celebration the "facts" of ordinary American life, each line of poetry a leaf of grass, each leaf a microcosm, his book one with Walt Whitman, and Walt, the representative man, one with the universe.

Thoreau was another born synecdochist, a better one than Emerson, because he was convinced, like Goethe, that nature is the *final* fact, that God culminates in the present moment and will never be more divine in all the ages. "I have travelled a great deal in Concord," he said, and his writings are a running record of the splendor he found in the commonplace. There is one passage in *Walden* which shows with remarkable vividness the way in which an ordinary fact could for him become an epiphany. This is the part of the chapter entitled "Spring" where he contemplates a frozen sandbank along the railroad as it melts in the warm spring sun. The "fact" with which he starts could hardly be more mundane—wet mud flowing down a hillside, and he begins with a quiet notation of what he sees, describing the mud forms with almost scientific detachment. They remind him of lava, lungs, bowels, excrements, coral, leopard's paws, birds' feet, ice crystals, the feathers and wings of birds, the thalluses of lichens, and most of all leaf forms of many kinds. As he hits upon the idea of leaf, his mind seems to undergo that Baudelairean shift to higher consciousness, and the leaf symbol, which had lain there all the time imbedded in the mud he brings to life, expanding it with play of the imagination until it fills the corners of the universe and includes the secret of renewal, birth, creation, the face of God Himself. "I am affected," he wrote, "as if in a peculiar sense I stood in the laboratory of the Artist who made the world and me—had come to where he was still at work sporting on this bank and with excess of energy strewing fresh designs about . . . Thus it seemed that this one hillside illustrated the principle of all the operations of Nature. The Maker of the earth but patented a leaf."

The organicism so prominent in Thoreau's leaf symbol is often a part of the symbolist synecdoche. Richard Wagner once told of how, in composing his opera *The Flying Dutchman*, he first wrote the words and music to the ballad which Senta sings in the second act. "Unconsciously," he wrote, "I deposited in this number the thematic germs of the entire score. It was a concentrated image of the whole drama as it outlined itself in my thoughts . . . When, finally, I passed on to composition, the thematic image which I had conceived opened out of its own accord, like a network over the whole score."[8] Wagner's image here is of a song which was like a seed or germ and which blossomed out under his composer's imagination into the full opera.

Coleridge's definition of the symbol has this same organic component: "It [the symbol] always partakes of the reality which it renders intelligible; and while it enunciates the whole, abides itself as a living part in that unity of which it is the representative." The Tiresias of Eliot's *The Wasteland* can serve as a good example of a synecdoche which is this kind of symbol. Eliot tells us in a note to the poem that even though Tiresias is a mere spectator and not a character in the poem, yet he is the poem's most important personage and unites all the rest. "Just as the one-eyed merchant, seller of currants, melts into the Phoenician Sailor, and the latter is not wholly distinct from Ferdinand Prince of Naples, so all the women are one woman, and the two sexes meet in Tiresias. What Tiresias *sees*, in fact, is the substance of the poem." Such a conception violates the most basic assumptions of the logical Western mind. Eliot asks that the reader of the poem accept Tiresias as the seer of ancient Greek myth, *and* as the contemporary center of perception, *and* as a woman, *and* as a man, *and* as all of the men and women in the poem. He asks, in a word, that the reader view Tiresias as a synecdoche which retains its discrete individuality in half a dozen mutually exclusive forms and yet at the same time expresses the collective meaning of the entire poem. To do this, the reader must abandon his modern discursive mind and think mythically, or in Keats' famous phrase, think with "negative capability"—that ability to rest in doubts and mysteries and uncertainties without any irritable reaching after fact and certainty.

Synecdochic meaning, of course, depends upon who is reading the synecdoche. A trained paleontologist can reconstruct an entire dinosaur from something which would appear to another person to be simply an old bone. But the symbolist poets have always assumed a great deal on the part of the reader, as these crisp lines from Pound's "Hugh Selwyn Mauberley" show:

120

The tea-rose tea-gown, etc.
Supplants the mousseline of Cos,
The Pianola "replaces"
Sappho's barbitos.

Christ follows Dionysus,
Phallic and ambrosial
Made way for macerations:
Caliban casts out Ariel.

The obscurity here is due to the severe reduction of the elliptical style and to the obliquity or remoteness of the allusions, but the symbolist trick of using the smallest possible particle to suggest a larger whole can easily be seen. "Tea-gown" and "mousseline," "Pianola" and "barbitos," "Christ" and "Dionysus," "Caliban" and "Ariel," each capsulizes a very complex area of meaning.

The opening lines of Kafka's strange short story, "The Hunter Gracchus," can illustrate still another kind of synecdoche and another kind of obscurity:

Two boys were sitting on the harbor wall playing with dice. A man was reading a newspaper on the steps of the monument resting in the shadow of a hero who was flourishing his sword on high. A girl was filling her bucket at the fountain. A fruit-seller was lying beside his scales, staring out to sea. Through the vacant window and door openings of a cafe one could see two men quite at the back drinking their wine. The proprietor was sitting at a table in front and dozing, a bark was silently making for the little harbor, as if borne by invisible means over the water. A man in a blue blouse climbed ashore and drew the rope through a ring. Behind the boatman two other men in dark coats with silver buttons carried a bier, on which, beneath a great flower-patterned tasseled silk cloth, a man was apparently lying.

The images in this passage, given in stark and unqualified simplicity, have the strange clarity of images in a dream, or in a painting by Delvaux or De Chirico. They exist in mutual isolation and unconcern in an eerie stasis, and as the story continues, a series of scenes and actions is unfolded which deepen the air of enigma. A flock of doves alight in the street and feed; one of them, big as a cock, flies up to a window-pane and pecks at it. The man lying on the bier under the patterned silk says he is dead, and yet he carries on a conversation with the mayor of the little town. There is no mistaking the distinctness of each particular with which the author has constructed his story, and yet no key is given, no solution to the mystery is suggested. Many of the images expand momentarily into larger meaning, only to be eclipsed by the expansion of some other image: none assumes a shape which will encompass the entire story.

We should mention, finally, a kind of particularity in symbolist literature which resembles the collage of visual art—that technique of glueing bits of wood or stone or string or cloth to a surface, often without an organizing topic or meaning. Joyce seems to be using such a technique in *Ulysses*, where innumerable details of life in Dublin on 16 June 1904 are laid out in bewildering and obfuscating profusion, sometimes without a detectable symbolic intent. William Carlos Williams' *Paterson*, with its often-stated principle, "no ideas but in things," uses this technique and combines anecdotes, bits of news stories, excerpts from old history books, songs, sermons, geological surveys, with lyric verse of the poet's own composition. On several occasions William said, "No symbolism will do," by which he apparently meant that no allegorical abstractions of the traditional sort would do. He carries to an extreme the symbolist identification of words and things. One of his abiding convictions was that life in modern America is polluted because the language is polluted—stale as a whale's breath from too much accumulation from the past. The office of the poet is to purify the language and thus the life it serves. He does this by reattaching words to things, by immersing himself in the filthy Passaic River, Williams' synecdoche for urbanized, industrialized America. The poet must use the indigenous, local materials of the spoiled cities and express these particulars with native, colloquial words. He must, in a word, observe with utmost rigor the principle of particularity.

As is well known, Williams was appalled when *The Wasteland* was published, exclaiming angrily that Eliot had set the whole thing back forty years by taking poetry back to the academy. Eliot's commitment to the past and to tradition was certainly plain enough, but so was his own desire to purify the language of the tribe in his own quite different way. Seen under the rubric of symbolism, the two look closer together than they are usually thought to be. A. N. Whitehead in his book *Symbolism*, describes two main parts to the basic phenomenon of "symbolic reference," the process by which symbols "mean" something beyond themselves. The first part of this process he called "presentational immediacy," by which he meant, roughly, the immediate impact of a thing upon the senses; the second part of the process he called "causal efficacy," by which he meant, roughly, the weight of the accumulated past of the object upon the present moment.[9] Williams was clearly devoted to "presentational immediacy," and Eliot to "causal efficacy," but both were true symbolists, and both were, after their separate fashion, synecdochists, practitioners of the principle of particularity.

IV

The Principle of Tensive Context: Meaning as Process

> I am what is around me.
> Wallace Stevens, *CP*, p. 86.

The synecdochic principle in symbolist writing is entangled with several other principles including the metamorphic shifting of forms and the idea of "field" or tensive context. This amalgam can be seen in a striking passage from E. E. Cummings' experimental play *Him*. At one point the main character, Him, reads from his notebook these reflections about the nature of the real world:

> These solidities and silences which we call "things" are not separate units of experience, but are poises, self-organising collections. There are no entities, no isolations, no abstractions; but there are departures, voyages, arrivals, contagions. I have seen an instant of consciousness as a heap of jackstraws. This heap is not inert; it is a kinesis fatally composed of countless mutually dependent stresses, a product-and-quotient of innumerable perfectly interrelated tensions. Tensions (by which any portion flowing through every other portion flowing through every other portion becomes the whole) are the technique and essence of Being.[10]

123

This passage nicely summarizes much of the modern symbolist view of reality, but we are particularly interested at this point in two parts of it: the idea of kinetic tension as the essence of reality, and the idea of one portion of a kinesis somehow *becoming* the whole.

Cummings' words run parallel to statements by the philosophers of symbolism: "Every actual thing," writes Alfred North Whitehead, "is something by reason of its activity; whereby its nature consists in its relevance to other things, and its individuality consists in its synthesis of other things so far as they are relevant to it."[11] Susanne Langer makes a similar statement when she describes meaning as a function of a term: "A function is a *pattern* viewed with reference to one special term round which it centers; this pattern emerges when we look at a given term *in its total relation to the other terms about it.*"[12] Charles Olson and others have made familiar the concept of a poem as a high-energy construct, analogous to a force field in physics, and Olson insists that poetry should be "composition by field."[13]

Every piece of literature is to some extent such a field, its separate elements creating an ambience in which each part necessarily energizes all others. And this means that an apparently insignificant part can at times achieve unusually high significance because of the special tensions created by a particular context. Wallace Stevens notes in one of the essays in *A Necessary Angel* the unusual poignance of the line from Wordsworth's "Michael": "And never lifted up a single stone." Outside the poem, he suggests, this line has only the most mundane significance; inside the poem, it carries all the terrible weight of the old man's grief and despair at the corruption and irretrievable loss of his only son. Because of the dynamics of poetic structure, the whole poem flows through this one part, which can thus be seen as a synecdoche for the entire poem.

This synecdochic phenomenon is much more important in a symbolist writing than in writing of other kinds because in symbolist writing the structural parameters are less specified. Narrative is often suppressed or implied rather than made explicit; the connections and transitions between parts of the writing are often omitted; the sign function of the words is diminished so that lines of reference to the real world are either blurred, made ambiguous or paradoxical, or reduced to a minimum. For these reasons, a symbolist writing, with its "clues and indirections" tends to be more self-referring than other kinds of writing. Its clues to meaning are more self-contained and the reader is perforce driven to the work itself for answers to his questions of meaning, and he naturally focuses on one main image, event, or character after another in his search for answers. And this means that he is forced to construe the poem again and again, funnelling the whole through one part after another in his attempt to discover its rational meanings, and this forces each of these separate parts in turn into a synecdochic role.

From Poe's time on, symbolists spoke of the didactic element as "heresy" and of an ideal "purity" in poetry, by which they meant that a poem should have a minimum of theme or idea or reference to the real world and should approach as nearly as possible the condition of music, which was seen to be the purest of the arts because the most self-referring. Mallarmé actually tried in some of his poems to give his words a notational value like that of music, and Flaubert in a letter to Louise Colet in Jan 1852 wrote of his desire to write a novel about nothing, "a book without attachments of any sort, which would hold of itself, through the inner strength of the style, as the earth sustains itself with no support in air, a book with almost no subject. Or at least an almost invisible subject, if possible."[14] Abstract expressionist painters like Jackson Pollock in the present century actually achieved "pure" painting with paint, canvas, style, and no subject matter. But in literary art this kind of "purity" is much more difficult, if not impossible, since words always carry some sign value, even if they are made-up words like "slithy toves" or "mimsy borogoves."

The symbolists saw music as the purest art because it seemed to them to be the most autonomous art; it was not *about* something, it *was* that something itself. But even though literature could not be made wholly pure, it turned out that there were ways in which it could be made to approach the autonomy of music. Through style, understood in its broadest sense to include structure, a reader might be forced to take a poem or a story, not for its message, but in its own terms, for *itself*. In a novel like Joyce's *Ulysses* or Faulkner's *The Sound and the Fury* or a poem like *The Wasteland* or *Paterson*, a reader must know well the overall design of the work before he can understand its individual parts, and paradoxically, he must know well the individual parts before he can grasp the overall design. What this means in simplest terms is that such a work can almost never be

125

understood in a single reading, no matter how painstaking, but must be read again and again until it has become in a true sense part of the reader's experience of life.

The style to which symbolist writers have turned to achieve this end often resembles the cubist techniques in painting, where a number of versions of the same object as seen from differing perspectives are presented simultaneously on the same surface, or where an object is broken into constituent elements and presented in distorted rearrangement. Joseph Frank has called such technique "spatial form" which, he says, demands a complete reorientation of the reader's attitude toward language. "Since the primary reference of any word-group is to something inside the poem itself," he argues, "language in modern poetry is really reflexive: the meaning-relationship is completed only by the simultaneous perception in space of word-groups which, when read consecutively in time, have no comprehensible relation to each other."[15] Benjy's section of *The Sound and the Fury* is incomprehensible until one is able to bring to bear upon any particular passage a detailed knowledge of the Compson family and of the characters and events of a forty-year span of time, and that means that the reader must have a comprehensive and intimate acquaintance with all parts of the novel, not only Benjy's section, but also Quentin's and Jason's, and Dilsey's.

We have suggested that the symbolist writing pulls a reader seductively on to discover its meaning, but always baffles any breakthrough to final understanding. The typical experience of this kind of writing is of a series of sudden flashes of illumination which promise to dissolve mystery with a clear shape of meaning, only to have each illumination fade because something in the configuration of the story or poem seems to have shifted so that the shape will no longer serve. Some part seems to lap over or must be left out, or there is a sudden impulse to see the poem in a wholly new way in accordance with a new flash of insight. This constant shifting of forms can lead a reader to frustration, if not despair, unless he learns the lesson of the pious pilgrim on the road to the holy city of Mecca, who despaired of reaching his longed-for goal because the road was difficult and his body enfeebled by age and sickness. One day his despair was lifted because he heard a voice say: "Mecca is the *road*; the road *is* Mecca!" The meaning of a symbolist poem is not in theme or idea but in the *experience* of the search for meaning, and much of our difficulty with this kind of writing is diminished if we cease to expect it to release a topical meaning, but learn to look upon it as a generator of a continuous flow of meaning, which means kinetically, as it is experienced by a particular reader. If the flow is stopped, analytical reason will simply burn a hole through this kind of literary fabric. Alice made this discovery in Lewis Carroll's *Through the Looking Glass*, when she found herself at one point in a quaint little shop:

> The shop seemed to be full of all manner of curious things—but the oddest part of it was, that whenever she looked hard at any shelf, to make out exactly what it had on it, that particular shelf was quite empty; though the others round it were crowded full as they could hold. "Things flow about here so!" she said at last.

Alice also discovered that one aspect of this flow was a metamorphic change of forms. A few moments earlier the quaint little shop had been a forest; and the long-nosed white sheep knitting behind the counter had been the white queen.

We have already seen that the Tiresias in Eliot's *The Wasteland* is the ancient seer of mythology, *and* the young man carbuncular, *and* the young stenographer whom he assaults sexually on the divan, *and* the Smyrna merchant, and all the other personages in the poem. Each of these images arises separately in the poem, but each is unstable and modulates into other forms. Melville's "Bartleby the Scrivener" presents the same problem: in spite of a relatively straightforward narrative and a certain realism in the Wall Street setting, very little remains stable. The story is polarized along an axis between the narrator and Bartleby, but both poles of this axis change continuously, and even on occasion merge into one another. Bartleby may be simply a pale, silent scrivener, a human derelict; or he may be a schizophrenic in a catatonic trance; or another incarnation of Christ; or a petulant nonconformist refusing to be "reasonable." One's reading of the story depends upon which of these one takes him to be, and equally important, which of a number of contradictory possibilities one takes the narrator to be, for he is equally unstable. He is "the boss" who benefits from and wields the power of an oppressive and ruthless society, but he is also indecisive and humane. His response to Bartleby runs a bewildering spectrum; he is at first indifferent to him;

then as Bartleby refuses to work or to leave, he tries to reason with him, to bribe him, to intimidate him, to evict him, and finally abandons him. The story suggests that he is like Pilate in questioning this man of sorrows, like Judas in betraying him to the law, like Peter in thrice denying him, but also like the Good Samaritan in caring for him.

In coming to terms with this story, which handle does one grasp? Melville has made it impossible to fix upon one to the exclusion of the others. One is moved to choose, but is given no indication as to what choice he should make. One can produce a stable reading of such a story only by accepting certain of these shifting facets of meaning to the exclusion of others. To take all into consideration means that one must accept like Alice the fact that "things flow about here so." And this means that at last we must accept in a symbolist writing the principle of flow, of metamorphic change, and a degree of paradox and ambiguity which no effort of mind can compel into focus.

V

The Principle of Variable Perspective

> There are as many points of view
> From which to regard her
> As there are sides to a round bottle.
> Wallace Stevens [OP, 136]

Once the individual imagination is granted the power of creating its own world, then there are going to be as many worlds as imaginations. "Fiction," said Conrad in the Preface to *The Nigger of the Narcissus*, "must be the appeal of one temperament to all the other innumerable temperaments whose subtle and restless power endows passing events with their true meaning, and creates the moral, the emotional atmosphere of the place and time." This Kantian principle, which has been accepted as a basic axiom of literary esthetics since early romantic times, has received confirmation in the present century from biological science. Dr. J. Z. Young, who is a specialist in the structure and function of the brain, asks the old question, what happens when a man who was born blind is operated on as an adult and suddenly receives

128

full vision? The answer, he says, is that on first using his eyes the man is almost certain to find the experience painful. He will experience a whirling mass of lights and colors but will be quite unable to recognize objects by sight. He will have no conception of space with objects in it, though if he closes his eyes and uses touch he will immediately know objects and their names. It may take years before he learns to *see* objects, because his brain has no experience, no models with which to compare his suddenly acquired sensation of vision. The cortex of the brain, Dr. Young explains, is like a great calculating machine which fits together parts of the input of our senses, and by comparing present input with previous inputs which left their mark on the brain, gives it rules by which to operate. And thus the brain of each of us does quite literally *create* his or her own world.[16]

Even without this kind of confirmation from science, poets since the beginning of the last century have shown a fascination with the act of perception, and symbolist poets in particular have made it a chief topic of their poems. Their interest in perception is related to their idea that words do not simply refer to reality, but that in fact they make reality, and that the impression made upon the mind by words is of the same order as the impression made upon the mind by things. Whitehead expresses this same idea: "There are no components of experience which are only symbols or only meanings . . . Why do we say that the word 'tree'—spoken or written—is a symbol to us for trees? Both the word itself and trees themselves enter into our experience on equal terms; and it would be just as sensible, viewing the question abstractedly, for trees to symbolize the word 'tree' as for the word to symbolize the trees."[17]

The symbolist poets tirelessly repeat ideas of this kind. This is Whitman in "A Song for Occupations":

All architecture is what you do to it when you look
    upon it,
(Did you think it was in the white or gray stone?
    or the lines of the arches and cornices?)

All music is what awakes from you when you are
    reminded by the instruments.
It is not the violins and the cornets, it is not
    the oboe nor the beating drums . . .

129

Strange and hard that paradox true I give,
Objects gross and the unseen soul are one.

This is Wallace Stevens, personifying his poetic imagination as a girl singing on the beach at Key West:

It was her voice that made
The sky acutest at its vanishing.
She measured to the hour its solitude.
She was the single artificer of the world
In which she sang. And when she sang. the sea,
Whatever self it had, became the self
That was her song, for she was the maker.[18]

And as the poet makes his world by words, so does the reader make his world by the words which the poet has given him, and the world he makes will be different from that of the poet or that of any other reader. "I look, you look, he looks; we look, ye look, they look," says Pip the wise fool in *Moby Dick*. Since the middle of the last century poets have tirelessly explored the many kinds of controlled narration, multiple perspective, and stream of consciousness which reflect this awareness of a reality which is relative to a particular consciousness. In *Ulysses* Joyce used eighteen major perspectives and an indefinite number of minor perspectives, and in "Thirteen Ways of Looking at a Blackbird" Wallace Stevens implies that there may be thirteen hundred more ways, or thirteen thousand.

This fascination with perspective is the reverse side of the symbolist's use of clues and indirections and his understanding of meaning as process. The reader in some sense always makes the meaning of any poem, as the innumerable readings of *Hamlet* bear witness, but the reader's perspective is of especial importance in a symbolist writing, where so much is deliberately left problematic. Meanings stream forth from the symbolist poem, but which meanings are available will depend radically upon the reader's own sensibility, and he will see only those meanings caught by his own lens or filter. In part he will see a version of himself reflected back from the story or poem: the Freudian will see Oedipus complex where the Marxist sees "surplus value"; the Jungian will see an archetype where the theologian sees a Christ-figure. When few elements of a poem are stable or certifiable, the field is open for the most extravagant intrusion of the reader's own subjectivity, and it is through this opening that the symbol-chaser breaks through to gambol about with freest abandon.

For many centuries the refrain in the liturgy, *Per omnia saecula saeculorum*, was translated, "Ever, world without end." In effect, the symbolist has altered that to, "Ever, *worlds* without end."

VI

The Principle of Presential Reality: Epiphany

It is actually there, in the life before us, every minute that we are listening, a rarest element—not in our imaginations, but there, there in fact.

William Carlos Williams,
Autobiography, 362

In direct conflict with the assumption that the mind makes the world by the act of perceiving it, the symbolist poets often testify to an experience of a presential reality, an underlying spirit in nature which *of itself* becomes manifest in objects and in the words of poems. Most of us who inherit Western culture still live by the dualism of Descartes which separates mind from matter, thinking subject from the objects of thought. And most of us are also positivists, tending to accept as "real" chiefly those aspects of reality which can be dealt with using the methods of physical science. We habitually view reality in visual, spatial terms; we convert sensory experience into solid, fixed objects which we locate *out there* in space. We allow these objects to have the measurable properties of mass, extension, and motion, and a life which is an invisible dance of atoms, but we reserve their other qualities such as color and smell to our own subjectivity.

These attitudes tend to suppress another kind of life which might be called the "felt presence" of some aspect of the real world. This can manifest itself in a person, a tree, a stone, a mountain, a cloud, an animal, a river. Primitive peoples commonly have a strong awareness of such presence or *mana*, which they understand to be a mysterious vital force present in differing degrees in all things, and which they perceive, as Cassirer said, *physiognomically*, under the aspect of

131

some particular emotional tone. This is the primitive sense of personal involvement and deep emotional awareness of the natural world which Lévy-Bruhl called the *participation mystique*, and which Martin Buber, in a well-known formulation, has described as the *I* becoming bound up in relation with some part of the world such that *It* becomes a *Thou*. In such a case a tree would cease to be simply a thing, but is accepted as having a kind of personhood. "The tree is no impression," writes Buber, "no play of my imagination, no value depending upon my mood; but it is bodied over against me and has to do with me, as I with it . . ."[19] Presence of this kind does not depend upon a projection of the ego upon the natural world, as in Ruskin's pathetic fallacy; it involves a flow of spiritual force the other way, from out there in, which is met by a flow from in here out, or perhaps more nearly, by an openness, a listening, a friendly receptivity.

In this concept of "presence" we are obviously verging upon the mythopoeic, if not the occult, but we are also at the very center of the symbolist esthetic. The poets themselves frequently acknowledge this kind of presential reality under a variety of names; Joyce called it the "radiance" or "epiphany" of an object. In both *Stephen Hero* and *Portrait of the Artist*, the narrator, Stephen, meditates a triad of terms from Thomas Aquinas, the three requisites for beauty—*integritas, consonantia, claritas*—integrity, symmetry (or harmony), and radiance. He has no difficulty with the first two qualities, which he says are discoverable by analysis, but *claritas* for a time gives him trouble, until it suddenly occurs to him that *claritas* is *quidditas*—radiance is whatness or particularity. This third quality is not discoverable by analytical reason but "leaps to us" from the object. "Its soul, its whatness," he says, "leaps to us from the vestment of its appearance. The soul of the commonest object, the structure of which is so adjusted [i.e. which has *consonantia*,] seems to us radiant. The object achieves its epiphany."[20]

Joyce's *quidditas*, in spite of its hint of Platonism, is not unlike the "thisness" of objects as seen in Gerard Manly Hopkins' theory of inscape, or the "concrete universal" upon which Goethe based his theory of the organic symbol, or Stevens' "vital, arrogant, fatal, dominant X," or William Carlos Williams' "radiant gist," or the "divine otherness" of D. H. Lawrence. Even Hawthorne registers an awareness of such presential reality in an unusual passage near the end of the thirty-fifth chapter of *The Marble Faun*: "There is a singular

132

effect oftentimes," he wrote, "when, out of the midst of engrossing thought and deep absorption, we suddenly look up, and catch a glimpse of external objects. We seem at such moments to look farther and deeper into them, than by any premeditated observation; it is as if they met our eyes alive, and with all their hidden meaning on the surface, but grew again inanimate and inscrutable the instant that they became aware of our glances." Rilke speaks of the same experience in one of the *Letters to Merline*, but advises that the vision is permitted only to those who can make a total commitment to the object for the time: "If a thing is to speak to you, you must regard it for a certain time *as the only one that exists*, as the one and only phenomenon which, thanks to your laborious and exclusive love, is now placed at the center of the Universe, and there, in that incomparable place, is this day attended by the Angels."[21] What Rilke urges here, it will be noted, is that the poet cultivate an attitude which Cassirer describes as the basic attitude of the primitive or mythic mind—that uncritical, passionate absorption in a single sensuous experience which causes everything around it to dwindle.[22]

"How is it," asked Whitman in his direct way, "that in all the serenity and lonesomeness of solitude away off here amid the hush of the forest . . . one is never entirely without the instinct of looking around . . . for somebody to appear or start up out of the earth, or from behind some tree or rock? Is it a lingering, inherited remains of man's primitive wariness, from the wild animals? or from his savage ancestry far back? It is not at all nervousness or fear. Seems as if something unknown were possibly lurking in those bushes, or solitary places. Nay it is quite certain there is—some vital unseen presence."[23]

This experience of presential reality is hardly the exclusive property of the symbolist poets; it was, for example, important to Wordsworth's early life and found striking expression in his poetry as in the famous passage from the *Prelude* where he tells of stealing a rowboat as a boy. He begins to row away from the shore when

> a huge peak, black and huge
> As if with voluntary power instinct
> Upreared its head. I struck and struck again,
> And growing still in stature the grim shape
> Towered up between me and the stars, and still,

For so it seemed, with purpose of its own
And measured motion like a living thing,
Strode after me.

Wordsworth tells of being deeply shaken by this experience and of turning back with trembling oars and returning the stolen boat to its mooring place, and for days afterward being troubled by "huge and mighty forms that do not live like living men," which moved slowly through his mind by day and troubled his dreams by night.

Poets have always felt such presences in the natural world, and the customary way of acknowledging them has been through use of the strong rhetorical figures of personification and apostrophe. But for the symbolist poet, this mysterious transection of the Universal in the particular, this glint and glimmer of Being shining forth from nature's humblest objects, has a special importance and a unique characteristic, because he sees it as the essential element of true poetry, a magic fire which can be caught by the poet's art and held in *words*. He believes that the words of a poem can contain the same presence, the same power of epiphany, as the objects in nature, that quite literally words can substitute for things. "There it was, word for word/ The poem that took the place of a mountain,"/ wrote Wallace Stevens.[24] And this is one of the reasons why the symbolist poet tends to look upon words as *things* having the same tangibility as other objects. In *Portrait of the Artist* Joyce describes Stephen walking in a lane "among heaps of dead language," and a little later shows him contemplating the word ivory, "which now shone in his brain, clearer and brighter than any ivory sawn from the mottled tusks of elephants."[25] Eliot spoke in "Burnt Norton" of the power of words, when given artistic form by the poet, of reaching out of the noise of time into the stillness of eternity, but added that in this effort, "words strain,/ Crack and sometimes break, under the burden,/ Under the tensions, slip, slide, perish,/ Decay with imprecision, will not stay in place."[26]

In an extraordinary passage from his *Autobiography*, William Carlos Williams makes a similar assumption that words are things, alive with an underlying presence, something he had called "the radiant gist" in *Paterson*. For Eliot and for Joyce it is chiefly the laborious precision of art, the *consonantia* bestowed upon words by the poet, which gives the artifact made of words its power of epiphany, but for Williams the presence is spontaneously there, implicit in the words as they are spoken by ordinary people, and the poet's office as much as anything else is to be open and receptive so as to register the words as they are spoken. He tells of catching glimpses as a practicing physician of this rare element in the unselected material of daily events, something which was carried in the words he heard his patients speak in his office or over the telephone. "The physician," he wrote, "enjoys a wonderful opportunity to actually witness the words being born. Their actual colors and shapes are laid before him carrying their tiny burdens, which he is privileged to take into his care with their unspoiled newness. He may see the difficulty with which they have been born and what they are destined to do. No one else is present but the speaker and ourselves, we have been the words' very parents. Nothing is more moving . . . For under that language to which we have been listening all our lives a new, more profound language, underlying all the dialectics, offers itself. It is what they call poetry . . . And it is the actual words as we hear them spoken under all circumstances, which contain it."[27]

He goes on to say that this rarest element is shy and jealous of exposure and shows itself only in the most particular of faces and never twice in the same way. Such presence makes itself felt in fleeting moments of impact upon the senses, and often upon senses other than sight; it comes, is vividly felt for a moment, and is gone, like Emily Dickinson's humming bird or Wallace Stevens' pheasant disappearing into the brush. And so we should connect this symbolist principle of presential reality not only with everything we have said about particularity but also with everything we have said about process and flow. Stevens spoke of presence as the "essential poem at the centre of things," something which is seen and known in the poems made of words:

> It is the huge, high harmony that sounds
> A little and a little, suddenly,
> By means of a separate sense. It is and it
> Is not and, therefore, is. In the instant of speech,
> The breadth of an accelerando moves,
> Captives the being, widens—and was there.[28]

In his acceptance of such presential reality and in his identification of words with things and with creative power, the symbolist poet is, in

135

effect, reaching around behind the Enlightenment to embrace mythic ways of seeing and saying which were dimmed by the advent of modern science, and it is in such practices, more than in the most assiduous use of allusions or paradigms from traditional myths, that the symbolist poet shows himself to be genuinely mythic. The symbolist epiphany effectively restores magic to a physical world from which it had seemed to be stripped away, and it gives, at least to the dedicated poet himself, a secular, esthetic version of the mystic experience which traditionally had been vouchsafed only to the religious. The poet's secret access to the vision is his imagination, which gives him the power to see what is actually before him as the world presents itself to his eyes every day. As Williams describes it in *Kora in Hell*, this power comes from a giving up of the arrogant will and an opening of the mind to the world of things. "A poet witnessing the chicory flower," he wrote, "and realizing its virtues of form and color so constructs his praise of it as to borrow no particle from right or left. He gives his poem over to the flower and its plant themselves, that they may benefit by those cooling winds of the imagination which thus returned upon them will refresh them at their task of saving the world."[29]

Here again that commitment to the single sensuous impression and the *participation mystique* of the mythopoeic mind, and if the remark sounds evangelical, it was meant to. Many symbolists, from Poe's time on, have described the poetic imagination as a means to salvation in a world darkened by materialism and literalism. The chicory flower, like other natural objects, has a saving vision to impart, but its life-giving epiphany can be seen only by that inner third eye of the imagination. And it is here that the words of poems achieve for the symbolist such unusual importance, because he believes that it is through the words of poems that the imagination of ordinary men can be energized and so can learn to open to receive the vision. So it is with poet as priest rather than entertainer that we have to do—poet as prophet rather than story-teller, poet as seer rather than singer, poet as magus rather than reporter—all of which may seem a bit overweening. But that is the way the symbolist poets have described themselves. Their mission they describe as nothing less than a program to change the mind of the Western world through the power of the creative Word.

[1] *The Medieval Mind*, 4th ed. (London, 1938), 2 vols., II, 69.

[2] William Faulkner, *Absalom, Absalom!* (New York, 1938), p. 143.

[3] *The Way Down and Out: The Occult in Symbolist Literature* (Ithaca, 1959).

[4] William Butler Yeats, "The Symbolism of Poetry," in *Essays and Introductions* (New York, 1961), p. 159.

[5] William K. Wimsatt and Monroe C. Beardsley, "The Structure of the 'Concrete Universal' in Literature," in *The Verbal Icon: Studies in the Meaning of Poetry* (Lexington, 1954). See also Philip Wheelwright's discussion of the concrete universal in chapter 3 of *The Burning Fountain* rev. ed. (Bloomington, 1968).

[6] Charles Baudelaire, *Oeuvres Completes*, ed. Y. G. Le Dantec rev. ed. (Paris, 1961), no. 17.

[7] *The Poetry of Experience* (New York, 1963), ch. 1.

[8] Quoted in Elie Siegmeister ed., *The Music Lover's Handbook* (New York, 1943), p. 493.

[9] *Symbolism: Its Meaning and Effect* (New York, 1954), p. 18.

[10] *Three Plays and a Ballet*, ed. George J. Firmage (New York, 1967), pp. 23-24.

[11] *Symbolism*, p. 26.

[12] *Philosophy in a New Key* (New York, 1958), p. 56.

[13] "Projective Verse," *Selected Writings* (New York, 1966), pp. 15-26.

[14] Quoted in Richard Ellmann and Charles Feidelson eds., *The Modern Tradition* (New York, 1965), p. 126.

[15] "Spatial Form in Modern Literature," *Sewanee Review*, 53 (1945), 221-240.

[16] *Doubt and Certainty in Science: A Biologist's Reflections On the Brain* (New York, 1960), pp. 10-11.

[17] *Symbolism*, pp. 11-12.

[18] "The Idea of Order at Key West," *Collected Poems* (New York, 1954), p. 129.

[19] Martin Buber, *I and Thou*, 2nd ed. (New York, 1958), p. 8.

[20] *Stephen Hero*, ed. Theodore Spencer, rev. ed. (New York, 1955), p. 213.

[21] Rainer Maria Rilke, *Letters to Merline*, transl. Violet M. MacDonald (London, 1952), p. 274.

[22] See *Language and Myth*, transl. Susanne K. Langer (New York, 1946), p. 57f.

[23] "Specimen Days," Feb. 22, 1877.

[24] *Collected Poems*, p. 512.

[25] *A Portrait of the Artist as a Young Man* (New York, 1957), pp. 178-179.

[26] *The Complete Poems and Plays*, 1909-1950 (New York, 1952), p. 121.

[27] *The Autobiography of William Carlos Williams* (New York, 1967), pp. 358-362.

[28] *Collected Poems*, p. 440.

[29] "Kora in Hell: Improvisations," *Imaginations*, ed. Webster Schott (New York, 1971), p. 19.

APPENDIX

What Is Symbolism? A Sheaf of Definitions

sym-bol n. [< Fr. & L.; Fr. *symbole*; L. *symbolus, symbolum*; Gr. *symbolon*, token, pledge, sign by which one infers a thing < *symballein*, to throw together, compare < *syn-*, together + *ballein*, to throw]. 1. something that stands for or represents another thing; especially, an object used to represent something abstract; emblem: as, the dove is a *symbol* of peace, the cross is the *symbol* of Christianity.

Webster's New World
Dictionary

No longer in a merely physical universe, man lives in a symbolic universe. Language, myth, art, and religion are parts of this universe. They are the varied threads which weave the symbolic net, the tangled web of human experience . . . Hence instead of defining man as an *animal rationale*, we should define him as an *animal symbolicum*.[1]

Ernst Cassirer

The principle of symbolism, with its universality, validity, and general applicability, is the magic word, the Open Sesame! giving access to the specifically human world, to the world of human culture.[2]

Ibid.

The human mind is functioning symbolically when some components of its experience elicit consciousness, beliefs, emotions, and usages,

139

respecting other components of its experience. The former set of components are the "symbols," and the latter set constitute the "meaning" of the symbols.[3]

Alfred North Whitehead

There are no components of experience which are only symbols or only meanings. The more usually symbolic reference is from the less primitive component as symbol to the more primitive as meaning.[4]

Ibid.

Why do we say that the word "tree"—spoken or written—is a symbol to us for trees? Both the word itself and trees themselves enter into our experience on equal terms; and it would be just as sensible, viewing the question abstractedly, for trees to symbolize the word "tree" as for the word to symbolize the trees.[5]

Ibid.

In the fundamental notion of symbolization—mystical, practical, or mathematical, it makes no difference—we have the keynote of all humanistic problems. In it lies a new conception of "mentality," that may illumine questions of life and consciousness, instead of obscuring them as traditional "scientific methods" have done.[6]

Susanne K. Langer

The older epistemological dyad [subject-object] is becoming replaced in contemporary philosophy, by an epistemological triad. Letting S stand for the knowing subject, L for the language (in the broadest possible sense) by which S undertakes symbolic expression, and O for the meant or sought for object, then the basic structure of any situation, so far as human beings can be aware of it or inquire about it, might be schematically represented thus:[7]

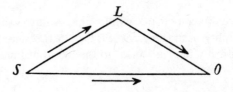

Philip Wheelwright

A symbol, in general, is a relatively stable and repeatable element of perceptual experience, standing for some larger meaning or set of meanings which cannot be given, or not fully given, in perceptual experience itself.[8]

Ibid.

Now what is the difference between a tensive symbol such as Mallarmé's faun, Crane's Bridge, and Yeat's Tower . . . and the kind of symbol that is discussed in *The Journal of Symbolic Logic* [i.e. a "steno" symbol like the Greek letter π]? The essential difference would appear to be two-fold. First, the logician is free . . . to stipulate what a symbol shall mean for the duration of an investigation or argument; secondly, the logician demands of his symbols, at least in principle, that they shall have a public exactitude, an uncompromising identity of reference for all who use them correctly . . . Tensive symbolizing, on the other hand, is alive and does not proceed by stipulation . . . nor is it ever perfectly exact.[9]

Ibid.

In a true symbol the particular represents the universal, not as a dream or shadow, but as the living and instantaneous revelation of the unfathomable.[10]

Johhann Wolfgang von Goethe

[A symbol] is characterized by a translucence of the special in the individual, or the general in the special, or of the universal in the general; above all, by the translucence of the eternal through and in the temporal. It always partakes of the reality which it renders intelligible; and while it enunciates the whole, abides itself as a living part in that unity of which it is the representative.[11]

Samuel Taylor Coleridge

True natural philosophy is comprized in the study of the science and language of *symbols*. The power delegated to nature is all in every part: and by symbol I mean, not a metaphor or allegory or any other figure of speech or form of fancy, but an actual and essential part of that, the whole of which it represents.[12]

Ibid.

Things admit of being used as symbols because nature is a symbol, in the whole, and in every part.[13]

Ralph Waldo Emerson

There is no fact in nature which does not carry the whole sense of nature; and the distinctions which we make in events and in affairs, of low and high, honest and base, disappear when nature is used as a symbol.[14]

Ibid.

We are symbols and inhabit symbols.[15]

Ibid.

A symbol is indeed the only possible expression of some invisible essence, a transparent lamp about a spiritual flame.[16]

William Butler Yeats

The scientific movement brought with it a literature, which was always tending to lose itself in externalities of all kinds, in opinion, in declamation, in picturesque writing, in word painting . . . and now writers have begun to dwell upon the element of evocation, of suggestion, upon what we call the symbolism in great writers.[17]

Ibid.

What was christened Symbolism can be summed up quite simply in the common intention of several poets (hostile to one another incidentally) to take back from music their own.[18]

W. Ramsey

It is on the lines of that spiritualising of the word, that perfecting of form in its capacity for allusion and suggestion, that confidence in the eternal correspondences between the visible and the invisible universe, which Mallarmé taught, and too intermittently practised, that literature must now move, if it is in any sense to move forward.[19]

Arthur Symons

The essence of Symbolism is its insistence on a world of ideal beauty, and its conviction that this is realised through art. The ecstasies which religion claims for the devout through prayer and contemplation are claimed by the Symbolist for the poet through the exercise of his craft.[20]

C. M. Bowra

Symbolism may be defined as an attempt by carefully studied means—a complicated association of ideas represented by a medley of metaphors—to communicate unique personal feelings.[21]

Edmund Wilson

The symbol originates in the split of existence, the confrontation and communication of an inner with an outer reality, whereby a meaning detaches itself from sheer existence.[22]

Erich Kahler

The symbol is something concrete and specific that is intended to convey something spiritual or general, either as an indicating sign, i.e. an act of pointing, or as an actual representation in which the dynamic division of the sign is abolished: that which points, that which it points to, and the act of pointing, have become one and the same.[23]

Ibid.

[Symbol] in this essay means any unit of any literary structure that can be isolated for critical attention. A word, a phrase, or an image used with some kind of special reference (which is what a symbol is usually taken to mean) are all symbol when they are distinguishable elements in critical analysis. Even the letters a writer spells his words with form a part of his symbolism . . . Criticism as a whole, in terms of this definition, would begin with, and largely consist of, the systematizing of literary symbolism.[24]

Northrop Frye

A symbol is a sort of excluded middle between what we know and what we do not know—or better, as Carlyle put it, a meeting point between the finite and the infinite.[25]

Harry Levin

The literary symbol proper is a key term, the center of many overlapping circles of metaphorical meaning.[26]

Charles Feidelson Jr.

143

[In answer to the question, what makes a phenomenon a symbol?] It may be impossible to give an answer to this question. This may be because the problem of symbolization is so extremely complicated; or symbolization may be a mental phenomenon of an absolutely fundamental and original nature. Thus is would be impossible to explain it as a function of any other mental processes.[27]

Hans Regnéll

A work of art is a single. indivisible symbol, although a highly articulated one; it is not, like a discourse (which may also be regarded as a single symbolic form), composite, analyzable into more elementary symbols . . . For language, spoken or written, is a *symbolism*, a system of symbols; a work of art is always a prime symbol.[28]

Susanne K. Langer

When the archetype manifests itself in the here and now of space and time, it can be perceived in some form by the conscious mind. Then we speak of a *symbol*. This means that every symbol is at the same time an archetype . . . The archetype is concentrated psychic energy, but the symbol provides the mode of manifestation by which the archetype becomes visible.[29]

Carl Gustav Jung

Insofar as a symbol is a living thing, it is an expression for something that cannot be characterized in any other or better way. The symbol is alive only so long as it is pregnant with meaning. But once its meaning has been born out of it, once that expression is found which formulates the thing sought . . . then the symbol is dead, and it becomes a conventional sign.[30]

Ibid.

As a uniter of opposites the symbol is a totality which can never be addressed only to one faculty in a man—his reason or intellect, for example—but always concerns our wholeness, touches and produces a resonance in all four of our functions at once [thought, feeling, senses, intuition].[31]

Ibid.

One of the important functions of symbols is to point toward and to communicate insights and wisdoms of life that cannot be otherwise

144

disclosed. This is the representational role of symbols, but it is not their major role . . . [There is a dimension of reality] for which the symbols are vehicles . . . Symbols in this sense are not merely means of communicating truth; they are the embodiments of reality itself.[32]

Ira Progoff

The literary symbol, an analogy for something unstated, consists of an articulation of verbal elements that, going beyond reference and the limits of discourse, embodies and offers a complex of feeling and thought. Not necessarily an image, this analogical embodiment may also be a rhythm, a juxtaposition, an action, a proposition, a structure, or a poem. One half of this peculiar analogy embodies the other, and the symbol is what is symbolizes.[33]

William York Tindall

Footnotes to Appendix

[1]*An Essay on Man* (New Haven, 1944), p. 25.
[2]*Ibid.*, p. 35.
[3]*Symbolism: Its Meaning and Effect* (New York, 1959), p. 7.
[4]*Ibid.*, p. 10.
[5]*Ibid.*, p. 11.
[6]*Philosophy in a New Key* 2nd ed. (New York, 1951), p. 32.
[7]*Metaphor and Reality* (Bloomington, 1962), p. 26.
[8]*Ibid.*, p. 92.
[9]*Ibid.*, p. 92-93.
[10]Quoted in Erich Heller, *The Disinherited Mind* (New York, 1959), p. 161.
[11]*The Statesman's Manual*, in *Complete Works of Samuel Taylor Coleridge*, ed. W. G. T. Shedd (New York, 1853), I, 437-438.
[12]*Ibid.*
[13]"The Poet," in *The Works of Ralph Waldo Emerson*, ed. James E. Cabot (Boston, 1883), 14 vols., III, 9-45.
[14]*Ibid.*
[15]*Ibid.*
[16]"William Blake and His Illustrations to the *Divine Comedy*," in *Essays and Introductions* (New York, 1961), p. 116.
[17]"The Symbolism of Poetry," in *Essays and Introductions*, p. 155.
[18]*Laforgue and the Ironic Inheritance* (New York, 1953), p. 7.

[19] *The Symbolist Movement in Literature* (London, 1899, rev. ed. 1919), p. 74-75.

[20] *The Heritage of Symbolism* (London, 1962), p. 5.

[21] *Axel's Castle: A Study in the Imaginative Literature of 1870-1930* (New York, 1931), p. 22-23.

[22] "The Nature of the Symbol," in Rollo May ed. *Symbolism in Religion and Literature* (New York, 1960), p. 53.

[23] *Ibid.*, p. 70.

[24] *Anatomy of Criticism* (New York, 1966), p. 71.

[25] *Symbolism in Fiction* (Charlottesville, 1956), p. 19.

[26] *Symbolism and American Literature* (Chicago, 1953), p. 64.

[27] *Symbolization and Fictional Reference* (Lund, 1949), p. 9.

[28] *Feeling and Form* (New York, 1953), p. 369.

[29] Jolande Jacobi, *Complex/Archetype/Symbol in the Psychology of C. G. Jung*, transl. Ralph Manheim (New York, 1959), pp. 74-75.

[30] *Ibid.*, p. 84-85.

[31] *Ibid.*, p. 88.

[32] *The Symbolic and the Real* (New York, 1963), pp. 211-212.

[33] *The Literary Symbol* (New York, 1955), p. 12.